Key Stage 2 English Comprehension

WORKBOOK 1

Dr Stephen C Curran

Edited by Andrea Richardson and Katrina MacKay

This book belongs to

ae®
TUITION

Accelerated Education Publications Ltd

Contents

Chapter One
BASIC APPROACHES TO TEXT

1. What is Comprehension?

English Comprehension involves reading and answering questions on a previously unseen passage of text. It is designed to test a child's literacy skills in three ways:

- **Reading** – to correctly decode (read) a passage, meaning that if a child read the text out loud the words would be correctly sounded. Reading the words correctly aids understanding as sound is linked to meaning.

- **Understanding** – to grasp the meaning of individual words (vocabulary), sentences, paragraphs and the overall meaning of the entire passage. This requires good spelling and vocabulary skills.

- **Writing** – the ability to parse (correctly order, spell and grammatically construct) proper sentences in answer to written questions in standard forms of testing. Multiple-choice tests do not require highly developed writing skills.

2. Categories of Text

All text is of two basic types: **Prose** or **Poetry**. They are distinct forms of language.

Prose

This is text that follows the ordinary grammatical structures and natural flow of everyday speech. It is used in all forms of normal communication and types of literature. It conveys thoughts and ideas through ordinary language and generates emotional response in a slower and more controlled manner.

Poetry

This is 'heightened language', meaning it is a highly concentrated form of text that is designed to evoke an immediate emotional response. Each word is carefully chosen for effect. It makes use of rhythm (meter), repetition, rhyme, symbolism through word and sound imagery, and allegorical (deeper meanings) or irony (double meanings).

Example: | Give a specimen of prose from a piece of classic literature.

This is an extract from *Peter Pan* by J. M. Barrie (1860-1937).

The fight was short and sharp. First to draw blood was John, who gallantly climbed into the boat and held Starkey. There was a fierce struggle, in which the cutlass was torn from the pirate's grasp. He wriggled overboard and John leapt after him. The dinghy drifted away.

Example: | Give a specimen of poetry from a piece of classic literature.

Here is a complete poem called *The Eagle* by Alfred Lord Tennyson (1809-1892).

He clasps the crag with crooked hands;
Close to the sun in lonely lands,
Ring'd with the azure world, he stands.

The wrinkled sea beneath him crawls;
He watches from his mountain walls,
And like a thunderbolt he falls.

Exercise 1: 1a   Identify whether these extracts of text are prose or poetry.

1) *Fog everywhere. Fog up the river, where it flows among green aits and meadows; fog down the river, where it rolls defiled among the tiers of shipping and the waterside pollutions of a great (and dirty) city. Fog on the Essex marshes, fog on the Kentish heights. Fog creeping into the cabooses of collier-brigs; fog lying out on the yards and hovering in the rigging of great ships; fog drooping on the gunwales of barges and small boats.*

Is this prose or poetry? ___Poetry___

2) *Rats!*
    They fought the dogs and killed the cats,
    And bit the babies in the cradles,
    And ate the cheeses out of the vats,
    And licked the soup from the cooks' own ladles.

Is this prose or poetry? _____

3) *Summer is gone with all its roses,*
    Its sun and perfumes and sweet flowers,
    Its warm air and refreshing showers,
    And even autumn closes.

Is this prose or poetry? _____

4) *On Christmas Eve I hung at the foot of my bed Bessie Bunter's black stocking, and always, I said, I would stay awake all the moonlit, snowlit night to hear the roof-alighting reindeer and see the hollied boot descend through the soot.*

    Is this prose or poetry? _____

5)

When you are old and grey and full of sleep,
And nodding by the fire, take down this book,
And slowly read, and dream of the soft look
Your eyes had once, and of their shadows deep

Is this prose or poetry? _____

3. Fiction or Non-fiction Prose

Prose breaks into two basic categories:
- **Fiction** is text that is not true and has been created from a person's imagination.
- **Non-fiction** is text that is true and is based upon real events.

Example: | Give a specimen of fiction from a piece of classic literature.

The Hare was once boasting of his speed before the other animals.
"I have never yet been beaten," said he, "when I put forth my full speed. I challenge any one here to race with me."
The Tortoise said quietly, "I accept your challenge."

This is fiction. It is an extract from *The Hare and the Tortoise* from Aesop's Fables (c. 620–564 BC).

Example: | Give a specimen of non-fiction from a piece of classic literature.

I was born at Shrewsbury on February 12th, 1809, and my earliest recollection goes back only to when I was a few months over four years old, when we went to near Abergele for sea-bathing, and I recollect some events and places there with some little distinctness.

This is non-fiction. It is an extract from *The Life and Letters of Charles Darwin* (1887).

Exercise 1: 1b

Identify whether these extracts of text are fiction or non-fiction.

6) *After a few hours the road began to be rough, and the walking grew so difficult that the Scarecrow often stumbled over the yellow bricks, which were here very uneven. Sometimes, indeed, they were broken or missing altogether, leaving holes that Toto jumped across and Dorothy walked around.*

Is this fiction or non-fiction? _____

7) *SATURDAY, JUNE 20, 1942*
Writing in a diary is a really strange experience for someone like me. Not only because I've never written anything before, but also because it seems to me that later on neither I nor anyone else will be interested in the musings of a thirteen-year-old schoolgirl. Oh well, it doesn't matter. I feel like writing, and I have an even greater need to get all kinds of things off my chest.

Is this fiction or non-fiction? _____

8) *Once upon a time there were four little rabbits, and their names were – Flopsy, Mopsy, Cotton-tail and Peter. They lived with their mother in a sandbank, underneath the root of a very big fir tree.*

Is this fiction or non-fiction? _____

9) *Vice-Admiral Nelson was shot by a French musketman at about 1.15pm on 21st October 1805, when the Battle of Trafalgar was at its height... After more than three hours of agony, Nelson finally died at about 4.30pm.*

Is this fiction or non-fiction? _____

10) *No one would have believed in the last years of the nineteenth century that this world was being watched keenly and closely by intelligences greater than man's and yet as mortal as his own; that as men busied themselves about their various concerns they were scrutinised and studied, perhaps almost as narrowly as a man with a microscope might scrutinise the transient creatures that swarm and multiply in a drop of water.*

Is this fiction or non-fiction? _____

4. Forms of Prose

The various **Forms of Prose** are not mutually exclusive. For example, we might find letters as part of a narrative or biography. A fictional story could be told through journal or diary entries. However, clarifying the various forms of prose is a helpful way of identifying particular types of literature and what we expect from it.

The various forms of prose are as follows:

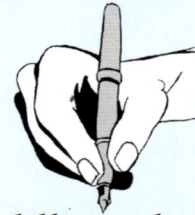

Narrative

This has a storyline or plot with a beginning, middle and end. The events of the story are often based around a main character and sometimes there is also a narrator who tells the story. It is usually fictional but can be based on true events such as historical fiction. It includes novels, short stories, fables, legends, myths, fantasy and fairy stories.

This is the opening piece of narrative from *The Secret Garden* by Frances Hodgson Burnett (1849-1924).

When Mary Lennox was sent to Misselthwaite Manor to live with her uncle everybody said she was the most disagreeable-looking child ever seen. It was true, too. She had a little thin face and a little thin body, thin light hair and a sour expression. Her hair was yellow, and her face was yellow because she had been born in India and had always been ill in one way or another.

Biography or Autobiography

This tells the story of someone's life from a personal perspective (autobiographical) or from the perspective of another writer (biographical).

This is an extract from explorer Captain James Cook's Journal dated 22nd June 1774.

The Conduct and aspect of these Islanders occasioned my giving it the Name of Savage Island, it lies in the Latitude of 19 degrees 1' Longitude 169 degrees 37' West, is about 11 Leagues in circuit, of a tolerable height and seemingly covered with wood amongst which were some Cocoa-nutt trees.

Persuasive Text

This kind of text attempts to convince a person to accept a particular view or opinion. It includes propaganda, advertisements, pamphlets and political or economic treatises such as *Das Kapital* by Karl Marx or *The Wealth of Nations* by Adam Smith.

This is an extract from the first speech delivered by Sir Winston Churchill as Prime Minister on May 10th 1940 to the House of Commons during the Second World War:

You ask, what is our policy? I can say: It is to wage war, by sea, land and air, with all our might and with all the strength that God can give us; to wage war against a monstrous tyranny, never surpassed in the dark, lamentable catalogue of human crime. That is our policy.

Factual Text

This kind of text imparts truthful information without bias or opinion. It can include textbooks, encyclopedias, leaflets, recipes, catalogues, directories and manuals.

This is an extract from *The World Almanac and Encyclopedia* of 1909.

Facts about the Earth: The superficial area of the Earth is estimated to be 196,550,000 square miles, of which 55,500,000 square miles are land and 141,050,000 square miles water. The diameter of the Earth at the equator is 7,926 miles, and at the poles, 7899 miles.

Reportage

This kind of text is factual but also conveys the bias or opinion of the writer. It includes any form of journalism such as newspapers, eyewitness accounts, magazines, journals, artistic criticism and travelogues.

This is a headline from *The New York Times*, dated July 21st 1969.

MEN WALK ON MOON
ASTRONAUTS LAND ON PLAIN; COLLECT ROCKS, PLANT FLAG
Voice from Moon: 'Eagle has landed'

Letters or E-mails

These are communications to another person or group. They can be formal (a letter of complaint to a company) or informal (a personal letter to a friend). Emails and text messages could now be included.

This is an extract from a letter sent by Grace Bedell, an 11-year-old girl to Abraham Lincoln on 15th October 1860 a few weeks before he was elected as president.

Dear Sir: My father has just come home from the fair and brought home your picture... I am a little girl only 11 years old, but I want you should be President of the United States... if you let your whiskers grow... you would look a great deal better for your face is so thin. All the ladies like whiskers and they... [would] vote for you and then you would be President.

Journals or Diaries

These can be fictional like *The Secret Diary of Adrian Mole*,

Aged 13¾ by Sue Townsend or from real life such as *The Diary of Anne Frank.*

This is an extract from the *Diaries of Charles Dodgson* or Lewis Carroll (1832-1898) where he speaks about the writing of his book *Alice in Wonderland.*

> *I do not know if 'Alice in Wonderland' was an original story – I was, at least, no conscious imitator in writing it – but I do know that, since it came out, something like a dozen story-books have appeared, on identically the same pattern. The path I timidly explored believing myself to be 'the first that ever burst into that silent sea' – is now a beaten high-road: all the way-side flowers have long ago been trampled into the dust: and it would be courting disaster for me to attempt that style again.*

Plays, Film Scripts or Interviews

These contain only the names of characters, their dialogue, stage directions and any descriptive action. This is an extract from *The Importance of Being Earnest* by Oscar Wilde.

> *(Algernon goes forward to meet them. Enter Lady Bracknell and Gwendolen.)*
> LADY BRACKNELL: Good afternoon, dear Algernon, I hope you are behaving very well.
> ALGERNON: I'm feeling very well Aunt Augusta.
> LADY BRACKNELL: That's not quite the same thing.
> In fact the two things rarely go together.

Example: | Identify the form of prose below.

WORLD'S GREATEST SEA TRAGEDY
TITANIC'S DEAD 1,500

With the $10,000,000 steamer Titanic lying two miles below the Ocean's surface, the number of dead today in the greatest marine disaster the world ever has known is estimated at 1,500. The huge liner foundered within four hours

---

after she crashed into the gigantic mountain of ice off the Newfoundland Banks and only her boats were found.

Answer: This form of prose is reportage as it is a front-page newspaper report from the *New York Journal*, April 16th 1912.

Exercise 1: 2

Identify the form of prose in the following extracts:

1)
NOW LOSE UP TO 20 POUNDS
on new weight-reducing plan that makes you
FEEL FULL WHILE DIETING
THE SECRET? Amazing new FASTABS
The wonder tablets that satisfy your appetite
completely, let you stick to any diet. Not a drug!

This form of prose is _____.

2) THE FLOWER GIRL: Garn! Oh do buy a flower off me, Captain. I can change half-a-crown. Take this for tuppence.
THE GENTLEMAN: Now don't be troublesome: there's a good girl (*trying his pockets*). I really haven't any change – Stop: here's three ha-pence, if that's any use to you (*he retreats to the other pillar*).
THE FLOWER GIRL: (*disappointed, but thinking three halfpence better than nothing*) Thank you, sir.

This form of prose is _____.

3) *I heard a confused noise about me; but in the posture I lay, I could see nothing except the sky. In a little time I felt something alive moving on my left leg, which advancing gently forward over my breast, came almost up to my chin; when, bending my eyes downwards as much as I could, I perceived it to be a human creature not six inches high…*

This form of prose is _____.

4)

WAR
11 a.m., September 3, 1939

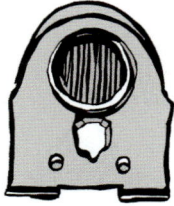

Great Britain and France are at war with Germany. We now fight against the blackest tyranny that has ever held men in bondage. We fight to defend, and to restore, freedom and justice on earth.

This form of prose is _____.

5) *2ⁿᵈ September 1666: Jane called up about three in the morning, to tell us of a great fire… in the City. So I rose, and slipped on my night-gown and went to her window, and thought it to be on the back side of Mark Lane at the farthest; but, being unused to such fires as followed, I thought it far enough off, and so went to bed again, and to sleep… By and by Jane comes and tells me that she hears that above 300 houses have been burned down tonight by the fire.*

This form of prose is _____.

6) *FOOTBALL, a game between two opposing sides played with a large inflated ball, which is propelled either by the feet alone or by both feet and hands… Regarding the origin of the game in Great Britain the Roman tradition has been generally accepted, although Irish antiquarians assert that a variety of football has been played in Ireland for over 2000 years.*

This form of prose is _____.

7) *Royal brother, having by God's will, for my sins I think, thrown myself into the power of the Queen my cousin, at whose hands I have suffered much for almost twenty years, I have finally been condemned to death by her and her Estates... I am to be executed like a criminal at eight in the morning... I scorn death and vow that I meet it innocent of any crime...*

This form of prose is _____.

8) *Wolfgang's genius impressed itself upon all. A writer of the time has recorded some of the tests to which he was put: "He plays from memory for hours. Give him a piece without bass, and he can add it without the aid of piano or violin. Give him an air for the violin and he will at once play it on the piano, adding the other parts. Sing a song and he will accompany it by ear varying the melody infinitely. Stretch a cloth over the keyboard and he plays with no less exactitude and speed".*

This form of prose is _____.

9) *It was in this scene of strife and bloodshed that the incidents we shall attempt to relate occurred, during the third year of the war which England and France last waged for the possession of a country that neither was destined to retain... Great Britain... had recently seen a chosen army led by a chief who had been selected from a crowd of trained warriors for his rare military endowments... routed by a handful of French and Indians.*

This form of prose is _____.

10)
VAPEX
INHALANT
FOR COLDS, CATARRH
AND INFLUENZA
A drop on our handkerchief
by day, on your pillow at night

Score

This form of prose is _____.

5. Narrative and Lyric Poetry

Poetry breaks into two broad categories:

1. **Narrative Poetry** tells a story or a sequence of connected events. Characters are propelled through a plot and the story is always told by a narrator. The poems can be long or short.

2. **Lyric Poetry** is non-narrative and expresses the ideas, thoughts or feelings of the speaker. Greek writers viewed a lyric as a song and a lyre accompanied it.

1. Narrative Poetry

This includes ballads, epic poems, lays and any form of poetry that tells a story about a character:

- **Ballads** tell a story in poetic form and are often sung. It is usually a folk tale or legend that tells a love story and often has a repeated refrain. This is an extract from the ballad *The Mermaid* – author unknown.

  'Twas Friday morn when we set sail,
  And we had not got far from land,
  When the Captain, he spied a lovely mermaid,
  With a comb and a glass in her hand.

- **Epic Poems** are long, serious poems, which tell the story of a heroic figure. Famous epic poems are *The Iliad* and *The Odyssey* by Homer and the epic poem *The Song of Hiawatha* by Henry Wadsworth Longfellow (1807-1882). Here is an extract from the poem, telling of the birth of Hiawatha:

  Thus was born my Hiawatha,
  Thus was born the child of wonder;
  But the daughter of Nokomis,
  Hiawatha's gentle mother,
  In her anguish died deserted...

- **Lay Poems** were long narrative poems that were often sung by medieval minstrels. Here are the opening lines of *The Lay of the Last Minstrel* by Sir Walter Scott (1771-1832):

  The way was long, the wind was cold.
  The minstrel was infirm and old;
  His wither'd cheek, and tresses gray,
  Seem'd to have known a better day;
  The harp, his sole remaining joy,
  Was carried by an orphan boy.

2. Lyric Poetry

This type of poetry directly expresses the ideas, thoughts and feelings of the poet about a subject. There are many forms of lyric poetry and here are some examples:

- A **Haiku** is a form of Japanese poetry composed of three unrhymed lines of five, seven and five syllables. Haiku poetry began in the sixteenth century and reflects on some aspect of nature and creates images. Here is an example:

  An old si/lent pond... (5 beats)
  A frog jumps in/to the pond, (7 beats)
  Splash! Si/lence a/gain. (5 beats)

- **Limericks** are short, humorous, nonsense poems consisting of five lines. Lines 1, 2 and 5 of a limerick have seven to ten syllables and rhyme with one another. Lines 3 and 4 have five to seven syllables and also rhyme with each other. Edward Lear (1812-1888) is famous for his nonsense limericks and here is an example:

  There was an Old Man in a tree,
  Who was horribly bored by a bee:
  When they said, 'Does is buzz?'
  He replied, 'Yes it does!'
  'It's a regular brute of a Bee!'

- **Odes** and **Sonnets** are also included. Odes are written in praise of something such as John Keats (1795-1821) *Ode to a Nightingale*. Sonnets are 'little songs' of 14 lines and are usually written in iambic pentameter (10 beats to a line).

  Shakespeare's many love sonnets are of the most famous. Here are the opening four lines of Shakespeare's *Sonnet 18*:

  Shall I compare thee to a summer's day?
  Thou art more lovely and more temperate:
  Rough winds do shake the darling buds of May,
  And summer's lease do hath all too short a date

Example: | Give a sample of narrative poetry.

The wind was a torrent of darkness among the gusty trees,
The moon was a ghostly galleon tossed upon cloudy seas,
The road was a ribbon of moonlight over the purple moor,
And the highwayman came riding –
　　　Riding – riding –
The highwayman came riding, up to the old inn-door.

This is narrative poetry. It is an opening verse of
The Highwayman by Alfred Noyes (1880-1958).

Example: | Give a sample of lyric poetry.

Music, when soft voices die,
Vibrates in the memory –
Odours, when sweet violets sicken,
Live within the sense they quicken.

This is lyric poetry. It is an extract from *Music When Soft Voices Die* by Percy Bysshe Shelley (1792-1822).

Exercise 1: 3   Identify whether the following extracts are narrative or lyric poetry:

1)　*The trees are in their autumn beauty,*
The woodland paths are dry,
Under the October twilight the water
Mirrors a still sky;
Upon the brimming water among the stones
Are nine and fifty swans.

This is _____ poetry.

2)

Half a league, half a league,
Half a league onward,
All in the valley of Death
Rode the six hundred.
"Forward, the Light Brigade!
Charge for the guns!" he said:
Into the valley of Death
Rode the six hundred.

This is _____ poetry.

3)   *A noiseless patient spider,*
I mark'd where on a little promontory it stood isolated,
Mark'd how to explore the vacant vast surrounding,
It launch'd forth filament, filament, filament, out of itself,
Ever unreeling them, ever tirelessly speeding them.

This is _____ poetry.

4)

"Is there anybody there?" said the Traveller,
Knocking on the moonlit door;
And his horse in the silence champed the grasses
Of the forest's ferny floor:
And a bird flew up out of the turret,
Above the Traveller's head:
And he smote upon the door again a second time;
"Is there anybody there?" he said.

This is _____ poetry.

5)   *There was an old person whose habits,*
Induced him to feed upon rabbits;
When he'd eaten eighteen,
He turned perfectly green,
Upon which he relinquished those habits.

This is _____ poetry.

6)

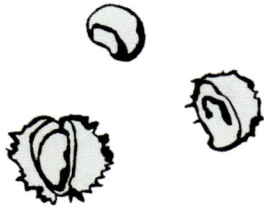

Autumn moonlight –
a worm digs silently
into the chestnut.

This is _____ poetry.

7)   *If you wake at midnight, and hear a horse's feet,*
      Don't go drawing back the blind, or looking in the street,
      Them that asks no questions isn't told a lie.
      Watch the wall, my darling, while the Gentlemen go by!
      Five and twenty ponies
      Trotting through the dark –
      Brandy for the Parson,
      'Baccy for the Clerk;
      Laces for a lady, letters for a spy,
      And watch the wall, my darling, while the Gentlemen go by!

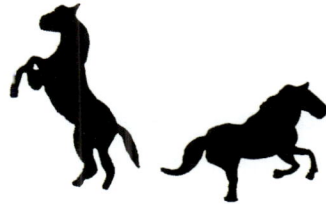

This is _____ poetry.

8)   *The glories of our blood and state*
      Are shadows, not substantial things;
      There is no armour against fate;
      Death lays his icy hand on kings:
      Sceptre and crown
      Must tumble down.
      And in the dust be equal made
      With the poor crooked scythe and spade.

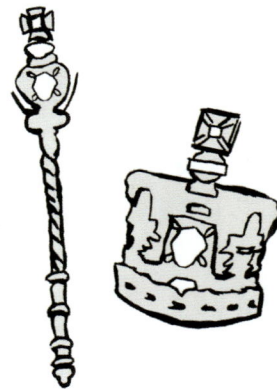

This is _____ poetry.

9)   *How doth the little crocodile*
      Improve his shining tail,
      And pour the waters of the Nile
      On every golden scale!

How cheerfully he seems to grin
How neatly spreads his claws,
And welcomes little fishes in,
With gently smiling jaws!

This is _____ poetry.

10) *We were schooner-rigged and rakish, with a long and lissome hull,*
And we flew the pretty colours of the cross-bones and the skull;
We'd a big black Jolly Roger flapping grimly at the fore,
And we sailed the Spanish Water in the happy days of yore.

We'd a long brass gun amidship, like a well-conducted ship.
We had each a brace of pistols and a cutlass at the hip;
It's a point which tells against us, and a fact to be deplored.
But we chased the goodly merchant-men and laid their ships aboard.

This is _____ poetry.

Score

Chapter Two
PROBING THE TEXT
1. The Purpose of the Writing

Another way of approaching a piece of text is to consider why it might have been written. This can aid understanding of the text and help us approach it in the right way. The reasons why people might write something cannot be easily narrowed down to one purpose. Many purposes are not mutually exclusive, i.e. an entertaining piece of text may also be descriptive or informative. However, many texts have only one overriding purpose and this can be easily identified.

There are five main reasons why someone might write a piece of text:

1. **To Entertain** – Many pieces of text are written mainly for the enjoyment of the reader. This means influencing the emotions of the reader. People can enjoy being scared, thrilled or intrigued as well as finding things funny. Literature that entertains can take many forms, e.g. stories, novels and poems.

This is a humorous and entertaining extract from 'How the Camel got his Hump' from the *Just So Stories* by Rudyard Kipling (1865-1936).

In the beginning of years, when the world was so new and all, and the Animals were just beginning to work for Man, there was a Camel, and he lived in the middle of a Howling Desert because he did not want to work; and besides, he was a Howler himself. So he ate sticks and thorns and tamarisks and milkweed and prickles, most 'scruciating idle; and when anybody spoke to him he said 'Humph!' Just 'Humph!' and no more.

2. **To Inform** – A piece of text is often written to educate or inform. This kind of text can convey an opinion or viewpoint but not necessarily, e.g. newspapers, magazines and journals carry opinions but an encyclopedia does not.

This is an extract from the entry on 'Cricket' in the *Encyclopedia Britannica* of 1911.

CRICKET – The game of cricket may be called the national summer pastime of the English race. The etymology of the word itself is the subject of much dispute. The Century Dictionary connects with Old French criquet, 'a stick used as a mark in the game of bowls,' and denies the connection with a staff. A claim has also been made for cricket, meaning a stool, from the stool at which the ball was bowled, while in the wardrobe account of King Edward I for the year 1300 is found an allusion to a game called creag.

3. **To Describe** – The focus of some pieces of text is description. It can be the description of a place, an event, a person or an object, e.g. travelogues, catalogues, diaries and journals often contain this type of text.

This is an extract from Dr. Beatty's eyewitness account of *The Death of Lord Nelson at the Battle of Trafalgar* (1807).

> *An hour and ten minutes... elapsed from the time of his lordship's being wounded, before Captain Hardy's... subsequent interview with him... They shook hands affectionately, and Lord Nelson said: 'Well Hardy, how goes the battle?'... 'Very well, my Lord,' replied Captain Hardy... 'I am a dead man, Hardy. It will all be over with me soon. My back is shot through.' Captain Hardy then returned on deck, and at parting shook hands again with his revered friend and commander.*

4. **To Explain** – This kind of text focuses either on helping the reader understand something or on how to do a particular task, e.g. textbooks, manuals, handbooks and leaflets.

This explanation of the light we see from the planets is from *Astronomy: A Popular Handbook* by Harold Jacoby (1913).

> *The planets are unlike the stars... The stars are self-luminous, incandescent; the planets are quite different, and give out no light of their own. They shine only by reflected light, which they receive from the sun. The light goes from the sun to the planet; illumines it; and then we see the planet by solar light, just as we see the objects in a room by reflected solar light, which we call daylight.*

5. **To Persuade** – A text that tries to persuade makes an argument or a case for some issue or product. It attempts to convince the reader that this particular point of view is the best one to adopt, e.g. advertising, propaganda and religious tracts.

This is a fictional advertisement for the services of an estate agent:

SELL IT QUICK ESTATE AGENTS
'THERE HAS NEVER BEEN A BETTER TIME TO SELL'
We have recently sold a house in your area and we have a large number of buyers still looking for houses just like yours. If you are thinking of selling or letting your property we would be delighted to discuss the matter with you and explain how we can offer you the best service.
We look forward to hearing from you soon.

Example: | Identify the main purpose of the text below:

I believe that no one could perceive where the vast body of water went; it seemed to lose itself in the earth, the opposite lip of the fissure into which it disappeared being only 80 feet distant. At least I did not comprehend it until, creeping with awe to the verge, I peered down into a large rent which had been made from bank to bank of the broad Zambesi, and saw that a stream of a thousand yards broad leaped down a hundred feet, and then became suddenly compressed into a space of fifteen or twenty yards. The entire falls are simply a crack made in a hard basaltic rock from the right to the left bank of the Zambesi, and then prolonged from the left bank away through the thirty or forty miles of hills.

The main purpose of this passage is to describe to the reader. It is an extract about David Livingston's discovery of Victoria Falls in 1855 from *Missionary Travels and Researches in South Africa* (1858) by Dr David Livingston.

Exercise 2: 1 Identify the main purpose of each of the following texts.

1) *June 28th 1838. I was awoken at four o'clock by the guns in the Park. Got up at seven, feeling strong and well. I dressed, having taken a little breakfast before I dressed and a little after. At ten I got into the state coach, and we began our Progress. It was a fine day, and the crowds of people exceeded what I had ever seen. Their good humour and excessive loyalty was beyond everything, and I really cannot say how proud I feel to be the Queen of such a nation.*

Identify the main purpose of this passage. Underline the correct answer.

     a) To persuade   b) To explain   c) To inform
     d) To entertain   e) To describe

2) *Below La Fère the river runs through a piece of open pastoral country; green opulent, loved by breeders; called the Golden Valley. In wide sweeps, and with a swift and equable gallop, the ceaseless stream of water visits and makes green the fields. Cows, and horses, and little humorous donkeys browse together in the meadows, and come down in troops to the riverside to drink. They make a strange feature in the landscape; above all when startled, and you see them galloping to and fro, with their incongruous forms and faces.*

Identify the main purpose of this passage. Underline the correct answer.

     a) To persuade   b) To explain   c) To inform
     d) To entertain   e) To describe

3) *The Big Baboon is found upon*
The plains of Cariboo:
He goes about with nothing on
(A shocking thing to do).

But if he dressed up respectably
And let his whiskers grow,
How like this Big Baboon would be
To Mister So-and-so!

Identify the main purpose of this passage. Underline the correct answer.

a) To persuade   b) To explain   c) To inform
d) To entertain   e) To describe

4) *The motto, "Be Prepared" means that the scout is always in a state of readiness in mind and body to do his duty. To be prepared in mind, by having disciplined himself to be obedient, and also by having thought out beforehand any accident or situation that may occur, so that he may know the right thing to do at the right moment, and be willing to do it. To be prepared in body by making himself strong and active and able to do the right thing at the right moment, and then to do it.*

Identify the main purpose of this passage. Underline the correct answer.

a) To persuade   b) To explain   c) To inform
d) To entertain   e) To describe

5) *I say to you today, my friends, that in spite of the difficulties and frustrations of the moment, I still have a dream. It is a dream deeply rooted in the American dream. I have a dream that one day this nation will rise up and live out the true meaning of its creed: "We hold these truths to be self evident: that all men are created equal."… I have a dream that my four children will one day live in a nation where they will not be judged by the colour of their skin but by the content of their character. I have a dream today.*

Identify the main purpose of this passage. Underline the correct answer.

a) To persuade   b) To explain   c) To inform
d) To entertain   e) To describe

6) *Alice was beginning to get very tired of sitting by her sister on the bank, and of having nothing to do: once or twice she had peeped into the book her sister was reading, but it had no pictures or conversations in it, 'and what is the use of a book,' thought Alice 'without pictures or conversations?' So she was considering in her own mind (as well as she could, for the hot day had made her feel very sleepy and stupid), whether the pleasure of making a daisy-chain would be worth the trouble of getting up and picking the daisies, when suddenly a white rabbit with pink eyes ran close by her.*

Identify the main purpose of this passage. Underline the correct answer.

   a) To persuade   b) To explain   c) To inform
   d) To entertain   e) To describe

7) *This morning the British Ambassador in Berlin handed the German Government a final note stating that, unless we heard from them by 11 o'clock that they were prepared at once to withdraw their troops from Poland, a state of war would exist between us. I have to tell you that no such undertaking has been received, and that consequently this country is at war with Germany.*

Identify the main purpose of this passage. Underline the correct answer.

   a) To persuade   b) To explain   c) To inform
   d) To entertain   e) To describe

8)   *ROAST WILD BOAR*
   Boar is cooked like this: sponge it clean and sprinkle with salt and roast cumin. Leave it to stand. The following day, roast it in the oven. When it is done, scatter with ground pepper and pour on the juice of the boar, honey, fish sauce, dessert wine and raisin wine.

Identify the main purpose of this passage. Underline the correct answer.

   a) To persuade   b) To explain   c) To inform
   d) To entertain   e) To describe

9)   **CHAMBERLAIN'S COUGH REMEDY**
                    A Safe Cough Medicine for Children
                In buying a cough remedy for children never be
        afraid to buy CHAMBERLAIN'S COUGH REMEDY. There is no
        danger from it, and relief is always sure to follow. It is intended
        especially for coughs, colds, croup and whooping cough, and is
        the best medicine in the world for these diseases. It is not only a
        certain cure for croup, but when given as soon as the croupy cough
        appears, will prevent the attack.

Identify the main purpose of this passage. Underline the correct answer.

   a) To persuade   b) To explain   c) To inform
   d) To entertain   e) To describe

10)   *He stooped a great deal and plodded along in a slow preoccupied
       manner, which made the bustling of London thoroughfares no
       very safe resort for him. He was dirtily and meanly dressed, in a
       threadbare coat, once blue, reaching to his ankles and buttoned
       to his chin, where in vanished the pale ghost of a collar. A piece
       of red cloth with which that phantom had been stiffened was now
       laid bare, and poked itself up at the back of the old man's neck,
       into a confusion of gray hair and rusty stock and buckle which
       altogether nearly poked his hat off. His trousers were so long
       and loose, and his shoes so clumsy and large, that he shuffled
       like an elephant; though how much of this was gait and how
       much trailing cloth and leather, no one could have told.*

Identify the main purpose of this passage. Underline the correct answer.

                                                        Score

   a) To persuade   b) To explain   c) To inform
   d) To entertain   e) To describe

2. Reading and Answering Questions

Reading Without 'Voicing'

It is important to gain as much as possible from a first read of the passage. As the speech centre of your brain controls so much of our thinking it is crucial to engage it. Mouthing the words of the passage without voicing them (speaking them out loud) is a useful technique and it stops the mind wandering through the first read through.

Prose normally only requires one proper read through using this technique. After this it is possible to scan the passage for answers.

Poetry should always be read more than once, as it is 'heightened language' (words or phrases often contain imagery and complex ideas). As poems are usually much shorter it means they can often be read two or three times.

Reading Actively

If you observe the following things when reading the passage it will mean you are reading in an active and alert manner and will notice far more. It will help you understand the nature of the subject matter. In other words, what the passage is about and any distinctive features it might have:

- The beginning and ending of the passage as ideas or themes are often summed up in these places
- Paragraphs tell you that groups of ideas or thoughts belong together, so try and sum up each paragraph in your mind as you read through
- Repeated words or phrases are often there to reinforce the main ideas
- Look for a title, a source reference or author's name as these things can give you clues about the text

- Underlining, marking or annotating the text helps you engage with the text

Answering Correctly

Unless a question is of a multiple choice type it must be answered in sentences. Use the question to structure your answer. For example:

Question: What day of the year is April Fools' Day?

Answer: April Fools' Day is on the 1st April every year.

Example: Read the following passage without 'voicing' and at the same time ensure you are reading actively. Answering correctly, write down in sentences what you think it is about and record any distinctive or special features it has.

Buck had accepted the rope with quiet dignity. To be sure, it was an unwonted performance: but he had learned to trust in men he knew, and to give them credit for a wisdom that outreached his own. But when the ends of the rope were placed in the stranger's hands, he growled menacingly. He had merely intimated his displeasure, in his pride believing that to intimate was to command. But to his surprise the rope tightened around his neck, shutting off his breath. In quick rage he sprang at the man, who met him halfway, grappled him close by the throat, and with a deft twist threw him over on his back. Then the rope tightened mercilessly, while Buck struggled in a fury, his tongue lolling out of his mouth and his great chest panting futilely. Never in all his life had he been so vilely treated, and never in all his life had he been so angry. But his strength ebbed, his eyes glazed, and he knew nothing when the train was flagged and the two men threw him into the baggage car.

An extract from *The Call of the Wild* by Jack London (1876-1916).

The Nature of the Subject Matter

This passage is about a dog called Buck, who resists being tethered by a stranger. In the struggle the stranger tightens the rope further and Buck nearly chokes. Eventually he is dumped in the baggage car of a train (three relevant sentences earns 3 marks).

It is distinctive because the hero of the story is a dog. The dog also appears to be able to think just like a human being (two relevant sentences earns 2 marks).

Exercise 2: 2

Read the following passages without 'voicing' them and at the same time ensure you are reading actively. Then write down what you think they are about and record what is distinctive or special about them.

Geppetto lived in a small ground-floor room that was only lighted from the staircase. The furniture could not have been simpler – a rickety chair, a poor bed, and a broken-down table... Geppetto took his tools and set to work to cut out and model his puppet. (4)

    "What name shall I give him?" he said to himself; "I think I will call him Pinocchio... Having found a name for his puppet he began to work in good earnest, and he first made his hair, then his forehead, and then his eyes. The eyes being finished, imagine (8) *his astonishment when he perceived that they moved and looked fixedly at him.*

    Geppetto, seeing himself stared at by those two wooden eyes, said in an angry voice: (12)

    "Wicked wooden eyes, why do you look at me?" No one answered.

He then proceeded to carve the nose, but no sooner had he made it than it began to grow. And it grew, and grew, (16)

and grew, until in a few minutes it had become an immense nose that seemed as if it would never end. Poor Geppetto tired himself out with cutting it off, but the more he cut and shortened it, the longer did that impertinent nose become!

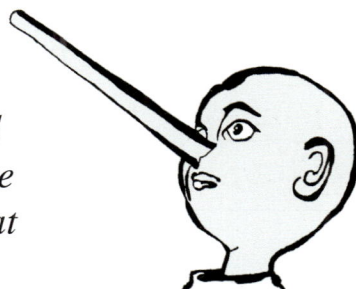

(20)

The mouth was not even completed when it began to laugh and deride him.

(24)

    "Stop laughing!" said Geppetto, provoked; but he might as well have spoken to the wall.

    "Stop laughing, I say!" he roared in a threatening tone. The mouth then ceased laughing, but put out its tongue as far as it would go…

(28)

Geppetto, at this insolent and derisive behavior felt sadder and more melancholy than he had ever been in his life before; and, turning to Pinocchio, he said to him:

(32)

    "You young rascal! You are not yet completed and you are already beginning to show want of respect to your father! That is bad, my boy, very bad!"
And he dried a tear.

(36)

This is an extract from *Pinocchio, The Tale of a Puppet* by Carlo Collodi (1826-1890).

Write your response in proper sentences. Each sentence should make one good point and can be credited with a mark. The beginning of the first sentence is provided.

The Nature of the Subject Matter

Score ☐

1-3) This passage is about _____

_____

_____

_____

_____ (3 marks)

4-5) It is distinctive because _____

_____

_____

_____ (2 marks)

LONDON'S DAY OF RAID WARNINGS
More Bombing Last Night
WANTONNESS OF THE GERMAN ATTACK
Premier to Broadcast This Evening

Following its third night of indiscriminate bombing – "the enemy has now thrown off all pretense of confining himself to military targets" states the Air Ministry, – London had five raid warnings yesterday. The first four, between 12.55pm and 5.55pm, were of short duration, and the enemy planes, which penetrated to the London area were apparently on reconnaissance.

The fifth warning was sounded at 8.15pm and was the prelude to another night-long raid.

The first few hours of the raid, as seen from the roof in the City, were uneventful. The German airmen had no fires to guide them and until 11.00pm confined their activities to the distant outskirts of London, from which gun flashes and occasional bomb explosions could be seen. Then the activity increased, and three bombs went off with a shattering roar in one district and three more in another district. Then all was quiet for a long time save for the rumble of distant guns.

An article from *The Manchester Guardian* – Wednesday 11th September 1940.

The Nature of the Subject Matter

6-8) This passage is about _____

_____

_____

_____

_____ (3 marks)

9-10) It is distinctive because _____

_____

_____

_____ (2 marks)

Chapter Three
ANALYSING PROSE
1. Five Key Questions to Address

A more probing analysis of the text can be achieved by using five basic questions. Each question has two parts to it:

1. Where does it take place?
- Identify the locations that are mentioned
- Give a brief description of these places

2. When does it take place?
- Identify the period of history, e.g. modern day or sometime in the past
- Specify the time of day, season, year or time period over which it takes place

3. Who is involved?
- Identify the key characters. Is there a 1st person (a character tells the story) or 3rd person (someone else tells the story) narrator?
- Briefly describe the key features of these characters

4. What happens?
- Summarise the main actions that occur
- Identify the key event that happens

5. Why does it happen?
- What does this event tell us about the story?
- Do these characters tell us anything about the story?

Example: Read this passage from *Treasure Island* by Robert Louis Stevenson (1850-1894) and use the five key questions: Where? When? Who? What? Why? in order to analyse the content of the passage.

At the Sign of the Spy-glass

When I had done breakfasting the squire gave me a note addressed to John Silver, at the sign of the Spy-glass, and told me I should easily find the place by following the line of the docks and keeping a bright (4) lookout for a little tavern with a large brass telescope for sign. I set off, overjoyed at this opportunity to see some more of the ships and seamen, and picked my way among a great crowd of (8) people and carts and bales, for the dock was now at its busiest, until I found the tavern in question.

It was a bright enough little place of entertainment. The sign was newly painted; the windows had neat red curtains; the (12) floor was cleanly sanded. There was a street on each side and an open door on both, which made the large, low room pretty clear to see in, in spite of clouds of tobacco smoke.

The customers were mostly seafaring men, and they talked so loudly that I hung at the door, almost afraid to enter. (16)

As I was waiting, a man came out of a side room, and at a glance I was sure he must be (20) Long John. His left leg was cut off close by the hip, and under the left shoulder he carried a crutch, which he managed with wonderful dexterity, hopping about upon it like a bird. He was very tall and strong, with a face as big as a ham – plain and pale, (24) but intelligent and smiling. Indeed, he seemed in the most cheerful spirits, whistling as he moved about among the tables, with a merry word or a slap on the shoulder for the more

favoured of his guests. (28)

Now, to tell you the truth, from the very first mention of Long John in Squire Trelawney's letter I had taken a fear in my mind that he might prove to be the very one-legged sailor whom I had watched for so long at the old Benbow. But one look at the man (32) *before me was enough. I had seen the captain, and Black Dog, and the blind man, Pew, and I thought I knew what a buccaneer was like – a very different creature, according to me, from this clean and pleasant-tempered landlord.* (36)

I plucked up courage at once, crossed the threshold, and walked right up to the man where he stood, propped on his crutch, talking to a customer.
"Mr. Silver, sir?" I asked, holding out the note. (40)
"Yes, my lad," said he; "such is my name, to be sure. And who may you be?" And then as he saw the squire's letter, he seemed to me to give something almost like a start.
"Oh!" said he, quite loud, and offering his hand. "I see. (44)
You are our new cabin-boy; pleased I am to see you."
And he took my hand in his large firm grasp.

1. Where does it take place?

- **Identify the locations that are mentioned** – The action takes place at the docks and in the old tavern, the Spy-glass.
- **Give a brief description of these places** – At the docks there are ships, crowds, sailors, bales and carts. The Spy-glass Inn is full of sailors talking loudly. It has a low roof, a sanded floor and red curtains in the windows.

2. When does it take place?

- **Identify the period of history, e.g. modern day or sometime in the past** – It is sometime in the 18th century as buccaneers are mentioned and there are old-fashioned docks.
- **Specify the time of day, season, year or time period over which it takes place** – It takes place at the busiest

point during the day, when the light is good and the ships are about to sail.

3. Who is involved?

- **Identify the key characters. Is there a 1st or 3rd person narrator?** – The 1st person narrator of the story (later named as Jim Hawkins) is to be new cabin boy. The other main character is Long John Silver who is the landlord of the Spy-glass Inn.

- **Briefly describe key features of these characters** – The narrator is the likely hero of the story. He is a young boy who is excited to go to sea. Long John Silver is said to be a buccaneer (a word often used of pirates). He only has one leg but can move swiftly about by using a crutch. He seems friendly and pleasant. Other characters include: Squire Trelawney who has written instructions for Jim (the narrator) about where to find Long John – the captain; Black Dog and the blind man Pew are also briefly mentioned.

4. What happens?

- **Summarise the main actions that occur** – The narrator makes his way through the crowds, following the line of the docks until he finds the Spy-glass inn. He is reticent to enter at first but when he does he is surprised to find he is welcomed warmly and reassuringly by Long John Silver.

- **What is the key event that takes place?** – The meeting of the new cabin boy (Jim Hawkins) and Long John Silver.

5. Why does it happen?

- **What does this event tell us about the story?** The opening narration gives us strong clues that this will be a swashbuckling adventure story that involves pirates and a long sea voyage.

- **Do these characters tell us anything about the story?** We are introduced to a key character, Long John Silver and perhaps the fact he is too nice, gives the reader a clue that all is not as it seems.

Exercise 3: 1 Analyse the following piece of text using the five key questions: Where? When? Who? What? and Why?

We crowded round and, over Miss Cathy's head, I had a peep at a dirty, ragged, black-haired child; big enough both to walk and talk: indeed it's face looked older than Catherine's yet, when it was set on its feet, it only stared around, and repeated (4) *over and over again some gibberish that nobody could understand. I was frightened, and Mrs Earnshaw was ready to fling it out of doors: she did fly up, asking how she could fashion to bring that gypsy brat into the house, when they had* (8) *their own bairns to feed and fend for? What he meant to do with it, and whether he were mad? The master tried to explain the matter; but he was really half-dead with fatigue, and all that I could make out, amongst her scolding, was a tale of his* (12) *seeing it starving, and houseless, and as good as dumb, in the streets of Liverpool; where he picked it up and inquired for its owner. Not a soul knew to whom it belonged, he said: and his money and being both limited, he thought it better to take it* (16) *home with him at once, than run into vain expenses there: because he was determined he would not leave it as he found it. Well, the conclusion was that my mistress grumbled herself calm; and Mr Earnshaw told me to wash it, and give it clean* (20) *things, and let it sleep with the children.*

This is an extract from *Wuthering Heights* by Emily Brontë (1818-1848).

Where does it take place?   Score [   ]

1-2) Identify the location or locations that are mentioned.

_____

_____ (2 marks)

3-4) Give a brief description of this place or places. _____

_____

_____

_____ (2 marks)

When does it take place?

5-6) Identify the period of history, e.g. modern day or

sometime in the past. _____

_____ (2 marks)

7-8) Specify the time of day, season, year or time period

over which it takes place. _____

_____ (2 marks)

Who is involved?

9-10) Identify the key characters. Is there a 1st person or 3rd

person narrator? _____

_____

_____ (2 marks)

11-12) Briefly describe the key features of these characters.

_____

_____

_____

_____

_____ (2 marks)

What happens?

13-14) Summarise the main actions that occur. _____

_____

_____

_____ (2 marks)

15-16) What is the key event that takes place? _____

_____

_____ (2 marks)

Why does it happen?

17-18) What does this event tell us about the story? _____

_____

_____

_____ (2 marks)

19-20) Do these characters tell us anything about the story?

_____

_____

_____

_____ (2 marks)

2. Investigating Prose Thoroughly

All we have learnt so far can now be drawn together into one approach to every piece of text. There are ten questions we can have in our minds when we read any piece of text.

The first five questions should be addressed on the initial read:

1) Is it fiction or it non-fiction?
2) What form of prose or poetry is it?

3) What is the purpose of the writing?
4) What is it about?
5) What is distinctive about it?

The second five questions should be used to probe the passage on the second read:

6) Where does it take place?
7) When does it take place?
8) Who is involved?
9) What happens?
10) Why does it happen?

Example: | Read this piece of text and answer the ten questions that follow:

For many months after this we continued to live on our island in uninterrupted harmony and happiness. Sometimes we went out a-fishing in the lagoon, and sometimes went a-hunting in the woods, or ascended to the mountain-top, by way of variety, (4)
although Peterkin always asserted that we went for the purpose of hailing any ship that might chance to heave in sight. But
I am certain that none of us wished to be delivered from our captivity, for we were extremely happy; and Peterkin used to (8)
say that, as we were very young, we should not feel the loss of a year or two. Peterkin, as I have said before, was thirteen years of age, Jack eighteen, and I fifteen. But Jack was very tall, strong, and manly for his age, and (12)
might easily have been mistaken for twenty.

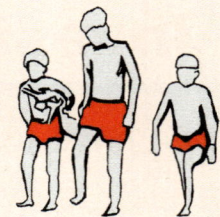

The climate was so beautiful that it seemed to be a perpetual summer, and as many of the fruit-trees continued to bear fruit and blossom all the year round, we never wanted for a plentiful supply (16)
of food. The hogs, too, seemed rather to increase than diminish, although Peterkin was very frequent in his attacks on them with

his spear. If at any time we failed in finding a drove, we had only to pay a visit to the plum tree before mentioned, where we always (20) *found a large family of them asleep under its branches.*

We employed ourselves very busily during this time in making various garments of cocoa-nut cloth, as those with which we had landed were beginning to be very (24) *ragged. Peterkin also succeeded in making excellent shoes out of the skin of the old hog, in the following manner. He first cut a piece of the hide, of an oblong form, a few inches longer than his foot. This he soaked in water, and while it* (28) *was wet he sewed up one end of it, so as to form a rough imitation of that part of the heel of a shoe where the seam is. This done, he bored a row of holes all round the edge of the piece of skin, through which a tough line was passed. Into the sewed-* (32) *up part of this shoe he thrust his heel; then, drawing the string tight, the edges rose up and overlapped his foot all round. It is true there were a great many ill-looking puckers in these shoes; but we found them very serviceable notwithstanding, and Jack* (36) *came at last to prefer them to his long boots.*

An extract from *The Coral Island* by Robert M Ballantyne (1825-1894).

Questions addressed from the initial read:

1) **Is it fiction or non-fiction?** This is fiction.

2) **What form of prose is it?** This is a piece of narrative prose.

3) **What is the purpose of the writing?** The purpose of the text is to entertain.

4) **What is it about?** This passage is about three boys who are marooned on a deserted island. Peterkin is thirteen, Jack is eighteen and the narrator of the story (later identified as Ralph) is fifteen years of age. They are happy on the island and have no desire to leave, as they are able to fish, hunt and forage for fruit.

5) What is distinctive about it? It is distinctive because it tells a story of three young and inexperienced boys and how they have been able to survive away from civilization. It also describes the island as an idyllic place with perpetual good weather and plentiful food.

Questions addressed by the more probing second read or scan through:

6) Where does it take place?

- **Identify the location or locations that are mentioned** – The deserted island and a number of places on it are mentioned. There is a lagoon, woods, the mountain-top and a plum tree.
- **Give a brief description of this place or places** – The climate of the island is temperate and many fruit trees bear blossom and fruit all year round. There are also plenty of hogs to hunt and fish to catch.

7) When does it take place?

- **Identify the period of history, e.g. modern day or sometime in the past** – It is likely to be more than 100 years ago as modern navigation would more easily locate people on an uninhabited island today.
- **Specify the time of day, season, year or time period over which it takes place** – No specific season is mentioned, but it seems like it is perpetual summer on the island because of the continual good weather.

8) Who is involved?

- **Identify the key characters. Is there a 1st or 3rd person narrator?** – They main characters are Peterkin, Jack and the 1st person narrator (Ralph).

- **Briefly describe key features of these characters** – Jack is eighteen and is tall, strong and manly. Peterkin is thirteen and seems adept at making things and hunting with a spear. The narrator (Ralph) is fifteen.

9) **What happens?**

- **Summarise the main actions that occur** – The activities of the boys include fishing, hunting, going up the mountain and making garments from cocoa-nut. Peterkin goes to the plum tree to hunt hogs and is also described making shoes out of old hog skin.

- **What is the key event that takes place?** – There is a detailed description of how Peterkin skilfully makes shoes for all of them.

10) **Why does it happen?**

- **What does this event or events tell us about the story?** It tells us how well the boys have adapted, the skills they have learnt and how happy they are to be on the island. As stories deal with problems, perhaps we sense this peace will soon be interrupted or broken.

- **Do these characters tell us anything about the story?** The boys are very resourceful and have learnt many things that will help them in the coming trials. The writer wants the reader to anticipate the coming danger and adventure.

Exercise 3: 2   Read this piece of text and answer the ten questions that follow:

The house where little Nell and her grandfather lived was one of those places where old and curious things were kept, one of those old houses which seem to crouch in odd corners of the town, and to hide their musty treasures from the public eye in jealousy and distrust. There were suits of mail standing like ghosts in armour, here and there; curious carvings   (4)

brought from monkish cloisters; rusty weapons of various kinds; (8)
distorted figures in china, and wood, and iron, and ivory;
tapestry, and strange furniture that might have been designed
in dreams; and in the old, dark, dismal rooms there lived alone
together the man and a child – his grandchild, Little Nell.
Solitary and dull as was her life, the innocent and cheerful spirit (12)
of the child found happiness in all things, and through the dim
rooms of the old curiosity shop Little Nell went singing, moving
with gay and lightsome step.

But gradually over the old man, whom she so tenderly loved, (16)
there stole a sad change. He became thoughtful, sad and wretched.
He had no sleep or rest but that which he took by day in his easy
chair; for every night, and all night long, he was away from home.
To the child it seemed that her grandfather's love for her (20)
increased, even with the hidden grief by which she saw him struck
down. And to see him sorrowful, and not to know the cause of his
sorrow; to see him growing pale and weak under his trouble of
mind, so weighed upon her gentle spirit that at times she felt as (24)
though her heart must break.

At last the time came when the old man's feeble frame could
bear up no longer against his hidden care. A raging fever seized
him, and, as he lay delirious or insensible through many weeks, (28)
Nell learned that the house, which sheltered them, was theirs no
longer; that in the future they would be very poor; that they
would scarcely have bread to eat. At length the old man began
to mend, but his mind was weakened. (32)

This is an extract from *Little Nell*, a short story by
Charles Dickens (1812-1870).

Score

1) **Is it fiction or non-fiction?** _____

2) **Underline the correct form of writing:**

a) Reportage   b) Lyric poetry   c) Narrative
d) Factual   e) Letter

3) What is the main purpose of the writing?
  Underline the correct answer.

    a) To persuade   b) To explain   c) To inform
    d) To entertain   e) To describe

4) This passage is about _____

_____

_____

5) It is distinctive because _____

_____

_____

Where does it take place?

6) Identify the location or locations that are mentioned.

_____

_____

7-8) Give a brief description of this place or places. _____

_____

_____

_____

_____ (2 marks)

When does it take place?

9) Identify the period of history, e.g. modern day or
sometime in the past. _____

_____

10) Specify the time of day, season, year or time period over
which it takes place. _____

_____

Who is involved?

11) Identify the key characters. Is there a 1st person or 3rd person narrator? _____

_____

_____

12-13) Briefly describe the key features of these characters.

_____

_____

_____

_____ (2 marks)

What happens?

14-15) Summarise the main actions that occur. _____

_____

_____

_____

_____ (2 marks)

16) What is the key event that takes place? _____

_____

Why does it happen?

17-18) What does this event tell us about the story? _____

_____

_____ (2 marks)

19-20) Do these characters tell us anything about the story?

_____

_____

_____

_____ (2 marks)

Chapter Four
ANALYSING POETRY
1. Approaches to Poetry

Comprehending and understanding poetry requires a different approach to prose. There are four aspects of poetry that need to be addressed:

Sound Devices • **Structure** • **Imagery** • **Meaning**

2. Poetic Sound Devices

There are five main ways of using the sound of words in poems to create effect:

1. **Alliteration** is the repetition of the same or similar consonant (hard) sounds at the beginning of words. For example the repetition of the *s* in the line:

   She sells seashells by the seashore.

2. **Consonance** is the repetition of consonant (hard) sounds at the ends of words. For example, in *God's Grandeur*, a poem by Gerard Manley Hopkins (1844-1889):

   And all is seared with trade; bleared smeared with toil;
   And wears man's smudge and shares man's smell: the soil

3. **Assonance** is the repetition or a pattern of similar vowel (soft) sounds in a line or at end of each line in a passage. For example, *The Bells*, a poem by Edgar Allan Poe (1809-1849):

   Hear the mellow wedding bells

4. **Onomatopoeia** refers to words or figures of speech

that imitate sounds. For example, *boom* sounds like an explosion or a cannon and *cock-a-doodle-do* sounds like the crowing of the farmyard cock. Here is a famous example of the effective use of onomatopoeic weapon sounds in this extract from *The Charge of the Heavy Brigade* by Alfred Lord Tennyson (1809-1892):

> <u>Fell</u> *like a cannon-shot,*
> <u>Burst</u> *like a thunderbolt,*
> <u>Crash'd</u> *like a hurricane*

5. **Anaphora** is the deliberate repetition of a word or phrase at the beginning of several successive verses, clauses or paragraphs. For example in this speech by John of Gaunt from *Richard II* by William Shakespeare (1564-1616) about England, we see the repeated use of *This* at the beginning of every line:

> <u>This</u> *royal throne of kings, this sceptred isle,*
> <u>This</u> *earth of majesty, this seat of Mars,*
> <u>This</u> *other Eden, demi-paradise,*
> <u>This</u> *fortress built by nature for herself.*

Example: Examine this famous poem closely and demonstrate how it displays each of the five poetic sound devices.

When I Heard the Learn'd Astronomer

When I heard the learn'd astronomer,	(1)
When the proofs, the figures, were ranged in columns	
before me,	(2)
When I was shown the charts and diagrams, to add,	
divide, and measure them,	(3)
When I sitting heard the astronomer where he lectured with	
much applause in the lecture-room,	(4)

How soon unaccountable I became tired and sick,   (5)
Till rising and gliding out I wander'd off by myself,   (6)
In the mystical moist night-air, and from time to time,   (7)
Look'd up in perfect silence at the stars.   (8)

By Walt Whitman (1819-1892).

This poem describes a person listening to a lecture on the facts and figures of astronomy, which he finds boring and dull. Eventually he is so irritated he leaves and examines the night sky and realises that no scientific explanation could ever capture the wonder of the stars in the universe.

The poem makes use of all five poetic sound devices:

1. **Alliteration** – The *m* sound is repeated in the 7th line: *In the mystical moist night-air* and the *s* sound is repeated in the final line: *silence at the stars*.

2. **Consonance** – This is used very effectively in line 2 where the *s* sound is repeated in *charts, figures, columns,* and also in line 3 where it is repeated in *charts* and *diagrams*. The words *them, room* and *time* are used at the end of the 3rd, 4th and 7th lines respectively and emphasise the *m* sound.

3. **Assonance** – Assonance occurs in line 6 with the repetition of the *i* sound in *rising* and *gliding*.

4. **Onomatopoeia** – The word *applause* in line 4 is related to the word *clap* by the use of the *app* sound. This word is onomatopoeic in origin. The word *sick* in line 5 sounds like somebody suddenly heaving and vomiting and is onomatopoeic.

5. **Anaphora** – The repetition of *When* or *When I* at the beginning of the first four lines is anaphoric.

Exercise 4: 1

Examine this poem closely and demonstrate how it displays each of the five poetic sound devices.

Song

When I am dead, my dearest,
Sing no sad songs for me;
Plant thou no roses at my head,
Nor shady cypress tree: (4)
Be the green grass above me
With showers and dewdrops wet;
And if thou wilt, remember,
And if thou wilt, forget. (8)

I shall not see the shadows,
I shall not feel the rain;
I shall not hear the nightingale
Sing on, as if in pain: (12)
And dreaming through the twilight
That doth not rise nor set,
Haply I may remember,
And haply may forget. (16)

By Christina Rossetti (1830-1894).

Score [ ]

1-2) Alliteration: _____

_____

_____

_____ (2 marks)

3-4) Assonance: _____

_____

_____

_____ (2 marks)

5-6) Consonance: _____

_____

_____

_____ (2 marks)

7-8) Onomatopoeia: _____

_____

_____ (2 marks)

9-10) Anaphora: _____

_____

_____

_____ (2 marks)

3. Poetic Structure

There are five elements of structure that are used to shape a poem:

1. Types of Verse

Formal Verse is poetry where there are rules on stanza length, meter or rhyme patterns. Well known forms include **Haiku** (5, 7 and 5 beats to a line) and **Blank Verse**, which is written in unrhymed iambic pentameter (10 beats or syllables to a line). Blank verse mimics the rhythms of ordinary speech. William Shakespeare wrote many of the speeches of his main characters in blank verse. This is the opening of his great play *Richard III*:

> Richard: *Now is the win/ter of our dis/con/tent* (10 beats)
>   *Made glo/rious sum/mer by this son of York* (10 beats)

Free Verse is a form of poetry composed of either rhymed or unrhymed lines that have no set fixed metrical pattern or beat. Modern 20th century poets used this to free themselves from the more rigid and traditional styles of earlier poets. These are the opening lines of *Song of Myself* by Walt Whitman (1819-1892):

> *I celebrate myself;*
> *And what I assume you shall assume;*
> *For every atom belonging to me, as good belongs to you.*

2. Stanzas

This is a series of lines placed into one unit and separated from other units by a blank line. In **Formal Verse** each stanza or verse will often have the same pattern of meter and rhyme. In **Free Verse** stanzas vary in length and meter. **Regular forms** of poetry have stanzas and **irregular forms** do not. The most common form of stanza is a quatrain – 4 lines. However, stanzas can be in couplets (2 lines), tercets (3 lines), quintets (5 lines), sestets (6 lines), septets (7 lines) and octaves (8 lines). This is a two stanza (in quatrains) poem in formal verse called *A Little Road Not Made of Man* by Emily Dickinson (1830-1886):

> *A little road not made of man,*
> *Enabled of the eye,*
> *Accessible to thill of bee,*
> *Or cart of butterfly.*
>
> *If town it have, beyond itself,*
> *'T is that I cannot say;*
> *I only sigh, – no vehicle*
> *Bears me along that way.*

3. Rhymes

Rhymes help draw attention to certain words or ideas. A poem in free verse has no rhymes. Rhymes occur in couplets, every other line, within a line and in many other patterns. This is an extract from *La Mer* by Oscar Wilde (1854-1900), which shows a rhyming couplet and a first and fourth line rhyme that can also be written as ABBA:

A white mist drifts across the <u>shrouds</u>,
A wild moon in this wintry <u>sky</u>
Gleams like an angry lion's <u>eye</u>
Out of a mane of tawny <u>clouds</u>.

4. Rhythm or Meter

Rhythm or Meter is important because it stirs up emotion. Words are made up of stressed and unstressed syllables and if carefully chosen, they give rhythm to a line. **Scansion** is the action of scanning a line of verse to determine its rhythm, making the writer's technique clear by indicating the stresses and the rhythm. In these examples the stressed syllables are underlined and we can build them into a poetic line with rhythm in three simple stages:

Stage 1: *<u>trai</u>/tor, be/<u>lieved</u>*
Stage 2: *His <u>day</u> of <u>death</u>*
Stage 3: *The <u>trai</u>/tor was <u>not</u> be/<u>lieved</u> and <u>faced</u> his <u>day</u> of <u>death</u>.*

The most common rhythm in English poetry is in **iambic pentameter**. This means there are five iambic feet or beats (sets of two syllables, one unstressed, one stressed) in each line. One short syllable is followed by a long syllable five times over as follows:

la-<u>LAH</u> la-<u>LAH</u> la-<u>LAH</u> la-<u>LAH</u> la-<u>LAH</u>

This occurs in the opening lines of *Romeo and Juliet* by William Shakespeare (1564-1616):

Two <u>house</u>/holds, <u>both</u> a/<u>like</u> in <u>dig</u>/ni/<u>ty</u>,
In <u>fair</u> Ve/<u>ro</u>/na, <u>where</u> we <u>lay</u> our <u>scene</u>

5. Punctuation and Line Breaks

Punctuation helps clarify meaning by indicating how the poem is to be read. Punctuation of different lengths creates rhythm and musicality:

Shortest – comma (**,**)
Slightly longer – semi-colon or dash (**;** or **–**)
Much Longer – colon (**:**)
Longest – full-stop (**.**)

A **Line Break** is created by a **Caesura**, which is any form of punctuation at the end of a line, or an **Enjambment**, which is a line ending with no punctuation, which means the reader tips over (like falling off a cliff) into the following line without a real pause.

Line Length gives poetry shape and rhythm. The various types are:

- Fixed length – Iambic pentameter (10 beats to a line) is an example of this type, but lines can be of other lengths too.

- Variable length – This occurs where there is a pattern of different line lengths within the stanza. It creates greater contrast between lines.

- No fixed length – This occurs in free verse where the length of line is determined by the subject matter.

In this extract from the poem, *Alas! This Is Not What I Thought Life Was* by Percy Bysshe Shelley (1792-1822), caesurae occur on lines 1, 2 and 4, an enjambment on line 3, along with mid-sentence punctuation and variable line-length:

Alas! this is not what I thought life was.
I knew that there were crimes and evil men,
Misery and hate; nor did I hope to pass
Untouched by suffering, through the rugged glen.

Example: Explain the structure of this poem using the five different structural elements of poetry.

Autumn Birds

The wild duck startles like a sudden thought,
And heron slow as if it might be caught.
The flopping crows on weary wings go by
And grey beard jackdaws noising as they fly. (4)
The crowds of starnels whizz and hurry by,
And darken like a clod the evening sky.
The larks like thunder rise and suthy round, (8)
Then drop and nestle in the stubble ground.
The wild swan hurries height and noises loud
With white neck peering to the evening cloud.
The weary rooks to distant woods are gone.
With lengths of tail the magpie winnows on (12)
To neighboring tree, and leaves the distant crow
While small birds nestle in the edge below.

By John Clare (1793-1864).

Notes on the text:
Line 5 – *Starnels* are starlings

John Clare is famous as a poet for his observations of the beauty and grandeur of nature. In this poem he graphically portrays the migration of birds to warmer climes.

The poem can be analysed using the five structural elements:

1. **Type of Verse** – This poem is a 14-line sonnet in formal verse.

2. **Stanzas** – There is only one stanza as a sonnet is always viewed as a complete whole.

3. **Rhymes** – Sonnets usually rhyme. This particular sonnet has rhyming couplets. For example, in lines 1 and 2 *thought* rhymes with *caught*. It can also be written as AA, BB, CC, DD, etc.

4. **Rhythm or Meter** – The poem makes use of iambic pentameter (10 beats or syllables to a line).

5. **Punctuation and Line Breaks** – As this poem is written in rhyming couplets, the caesurae at the end of the second of the two lines finishes with a full stop right down to line 10. The first of each of the two lines ends with commas except where there are enjambments at the end of lines 3, 9, 12 and 13. The iambic pentameter dictates that all the lines are of fixed length (10 beats to a line).

Exercise 4: 2 Explain the structure of this poem using the five different structural elements of poetry.

Only in Sleep

Only in sleep I see their faces,
Children I played with when I was a child,
Louise comes back with her brown hair braided,
Annie with ringlets warm and wild. (4)

Only in sleep Time is forgotten –
What may have come to them, who can know?
Yet we played last night as long ago,
And the doll-house stood at the turn of the stair. (8)

The years had not sharpened their smooth round faces,
I met their eyes and found them mild –
Do they, too, dream of me, I wonder,
And for them am I too a child? (12)

By Sarah Teasdale (1884-1933).

ae

The poet describes how she only remembers her childhood when she dreams. Time melts away and the faces of her young friends and the details of her earlier life come flooding back. She wonders if her adult friends still dream of her as a child too.

Score ☐

1-2) Type of Verse: _____

_____

_____ (2 marks)

3-4) Stanzas: _____

_____

_____ (2 marks)

5-6) Rhymes: _____

_____

_____ (2 marks)

7-8) Rhythm or Meter: _____

_____

_____ (2 marks)

9-10) Punctuation and Line Breaks: _____

_____

_____ (2 marks)

4. Poetic Imagery

Imagery is a way of conveying meaning and emotion speedily because it uses figurative or symbolic language. The brain understands images very quickly. This extract from *I Wandered Lonely as a Cloud* by William Wordsworth (1770-1850) clearly indicates how the poet feels:

I wandered lonely as a cloud
That floats on high o'er vales and hills,
When all at once I saw a crowd,
A host, of golden daffodils;
Beside the lake, beneath the trees,
Fluttering and dancing in the breeze.

There are five kinds of poetic figurative language that create imagery:

1. A **Metaphor** is a figure of speech that compares seemingly unlike objects. An example of a metaphor would be *drowning in debt*. If a poem is one long extended metaphor it is called an **allegory**. One of the most famous, the epic poem, *The Faerie Queene* by Edmund Spenser (1552-1599) is a tale about knights in medieval times on a journey in a fairy land that has a pure queen. This was really a poem in praise of Queen Elizabeth I. However, most poems just have metaphors within them. An example occurs in William Shakespeare's great play, *As you Like It*. The character Jaques compares the world to a stage and describes its people as actors:

   All the world's a stage,
   And all the men and women merely players:
   They have their exits and their entrances;
   And one man in his time plays many parts,
   His acts being seven ages.

2. A **Simile** is a figure of speech in which two things are compared using the word *as* or *like*. This draws attention to similarities between two things that are seemingly dissimilar. An example of a simile would be *a fleece as white as snow* or this extract from an unknown poet:

   Friends are <u>like</u> chocolate cake
   You can never have too many.

3. **Personification** is a kind of metaphor, and it means to speak of an impersonal thing, such as a season, a natural element, a country, or any object as though it were a person. An example would be, *lightning danced across the sky*. In this extract from *Two Sunflowers Move in the Yellow Room* by William Blake (1757-1827), we can see the poem is built around the idea of personification:

> *"Ah, William, we're weary of the weather."*
> *Said the sunflowers, shining with dew.*
> *"Our travelling habits have tired us.*
> *Can you give us a room with a view?"*

4. **Symbols** are images which convey ideas effectively. In this extract from *A Red, Red Rose* by Robert Burns (1759-1796), the symbol of the *rose* and then the *melody* represents the feeling of love:

> *O, my love's like a red, red rose*
> *That's newly sprung in June;*
> *O, my love's like the melody*
> *That's sweetly played in tune.*

5. **Hyperbole** is a description that is exaggerated for emphasis. It is often used in everyday language. For example someone might say, *I'm so hungry I could eat a horse*. An example of hyperbole occurs in William Shakespeare's play *Macbeth,* when Macbeth complains in an exaggerated way of the blood on his hands after murdering King Duncan:

> *Will all great Neptune's ocean wash this blood*
> *Clean from my hand? No. This my hand will rather*
> *The multitudinous seas incarnadine,*
> *Making the green one red.*

Example: Explain how the five kinds of poetic figurative language create imagery in this famous poem.

Upon Westminster Bridge

Earth has not any thing to show more fair:
Dull would he be of soul who could pass by
A sight so touching in its majesty:
This City now doth like a garment wear　　　　　(4)
The beauty of the morning; silent, bare,
Ships, towers, domes, theatres, and temples lie
Open unto the fields, and to the sky;
All bright and glittering in the smokeless air.　　(8)
Never did sun more beautifully steep
In his first splendor valley, rock, or hill;
Ne'er saw I, never felt, a calm so deep!
The river glideth at his own sweet will:　　　　(12)
Dear God! the very houses seem asleep;
And all that mighty heart is lying still!

By William Wordsworth (1770-1850).

This great poem describes the City of London on the morning of September 3ʳᵈ 1803. It is a 14-line sonnet in iambic pentameter (10 beats to a line). It contains all five types of poetic figurative language that create imagery:

1. **Metaphor** – London is compared to a *mighty heart* in line 14. Also, in line 1, *Earth has not anything to show more fair* infers that even the beauty of a woman, commonly described as *fair* in former times, does not in any way match this incredible sight.

2. **Simile** – There is only one simile indicated by the use of like in line 4: *This City now doth <u>like</u> a garment wear The beauty of the morning* etc.

3. **Personification** – The following four quotes show there is personification. In line 4, *This City now doth like a garment wear* – the city wears clothes like a person; in lines 9-10, *Never did sun more beautifully steep In <u>his</u> first splendor valley, rock, or hill* – The personal pronoun *his* is used for the sun; in line 12, *The river glideth at <u>his</u> own sweet will* – the river is also referred to with the personal pronoun *his*. The river is also described as having the choice or *will* to *glide* by itself; in line 14, the city also has a *mighty heart,* which beats just like a human being.

4. **Symbols** – *The very houses seem asleep* in line 13 is symbolic of the calm and peaceful state of the city. The *heart* is a symbol of the industrial and commercial life of the great city, which for the moment pulses slowly but retains its great power and will become active when day breaks.

5. **Hyperbole** – The poet uses exaggeration to get across his message. In lines 1-3 he claims in a great burst of feeling that there is nothing *more fair* than this sight of *majesty* and he who cannot understand it is simply *dull*. He continues to exaggerate for effect when he claims, in line 9, *Never did sun more beautifully steep* and in line 11, *Ne'er saw I, never felt a calm so deep.* In both cases the word *Never* is an exaggeration to create effect.

Exercise 4: 3

Examine how the five kinds of figurative language create imagery in this famous poem.

A bird came down the walk

A bird came down the walk:
He did not know I saw;
He bit an angle-worm in halves
And ate the fellow, raw. (4)

And then he drank a dew
From a convenient grass,
And then hopped sidewise to the wall
To let a beetle pass. (8)

He glanced with rapid eyes
That hurried all abroad, –
They looked like frightened beads, I thought
He stirred his velvet head (12)

Like one in danger; cautious,
I offered him a crumb,
And he unrolled his feathers
And rowed him softer home (16)

Than oars divide the ocean,
Too silver for a seam,
Or butterflies, off banks of noon
Leap, Plashless, as they swim. (20)

By Emily Dickinson (1830-1886). **Score** ☐

Notes on the text:
Line 20 – *Plashless* means without a splash

1-2) Metaphor: _____

_____ (2 marks)

3-4) Personification: _____

_____ (2 marks)

5-6) Simile: _____

_____

_____ (2 marks)

7-8) Symbols: _____

_____

_____ (2 marks)

9-10) Hyperbole: _____

_____

_____ (2 marks)

5. Poetic Meaning

When exploring the meaning of a poem there are five tools that can be applied:

1. **Subject** – This is the topic or issue the poem is dealing with. For instance, it could be about any number of subjects such as love, death, family, nature, youth or war. This extract from the poem *All Nature has a Feeling* by John Clare (1793-1864) clearly states in line 1 that its subject is nature and how its beauty can uplift the human spirit:

   > *All nature has a feeling: woods, fields, brooks*
   > *Are life eternal: and in silence they*
   > *Speak happiness beyond the reach of books;*

2. **Mood** – This is the feeling or atmosphere conveyed by the poem. For example, it may be a feeling of love, doom, compassion, fear, pride, chaos or peace. This short anonymous poem, *He is not Lost our Dearest*

Love, recalls the death of a loved one and conveys a feeling of sadness and grief:

> *He is not lost our dearest love,*
> *Nor has he travelled far,*
> *Just stepped inside home's loveliest room*
> *And left the door ajar.*

3. **Tone** – This consists of the poet's attitude towards their subject matter. For instance they may be angry, critical, cynical, depressed or amused about the subject. This can include **dramatic irony**, where the author creates an expectation in the poem, but the outcome is very different for the characters. For example in the *Rime of the Ancient Mariner,* by Samuel Taylor Coleridge (1772-1834), the author points out that although the thirsty sailors can see an ocean full of water, they cannot drink salty seawater:

> *Water, water, every where,*
> *And all the boards did shrink;*
> *Water, water, every where,*
> *Nor any drop to drink.*

William Blake (1757-1827) was a 19th century poet who showed great concern for the plight for the poor. These are the opening two stanzas of Blake's critical poem, *Songs of Innocence: The Chimney Sweeper* where he describes the conditions of these mistreated children. He uses **dramatic irony** in the second stanza. The child is told that the soot can no longer spoil his white hair if it is shaved off. This trivial issue is set against the gruesome fact that little Tom's life will be in mortal danger every day as he sweeps chimneys:

When my mother died I was very young,
And my father sold me while yet my tongue
Could scarcely cry 'weep! 'weep! 'weep! 'weep!
So your chimneys I sweep, and in soot I sleep ...

There's little Tom Dacre, who cried when his head,
That curled like a lamb's back, was shaved: so I said,
"Hush, Tom! never mind it, for when your head's bare,
You know that the soot cannot spoil your white hair."

4. **Theme** – This is what a poet is trying to say or the overall message of a poem. The theme is often contained in key lines at the beginning or the end of the poem. It can be repeated a number of times to emphasise the point. The theme of this short poem by Palladas, a 4th century Greek poet, translated by William Roger Paton (1857-1921) is contained in the title, *Contentment in Old Age*:

The women mock me for being old,
Bidding me look at the wreck of my years in the mirror.
But I, as I approach the end of my life,
Care not whether I have white hair or black,
And with sweet-scented ointments
And crowns of lovely flowers and wine
I make heavy care to cease.

5. **Moral** – If a poem tries to teach a lesson about what is right by using a story, some information or experience, it has a moral. An example of a moral that might emanate from the poem is to *respect your elders* or that *good always overcomes evil*. This short poem, *Happy Thought* by Robert Louis Stevenson (1850-1894), gives a line of information and then bases a simple moral upon it:

The world is so full of a number of things,
I'm sure we should be as happy as kings.

Example: | Examine this poem closely and use the five tools to express its meaning.

Dulce Et Decorum Est

Bent double, like old beggars under sacks,
Knock-kneed, coughing like hags, we cursed through sludge,
Till on the haunting flares we turned our backs
And towards our distant rest began to trudge.   (4)
Men marched asleep. Many had lost their boots
But limped on, blood-shod. All went lame; all blind;
Drunk with fatigue; deaf even to the hoots
Of disappointed shells that dropped behind.   (8)

GAS! Gas! Quick, boys! – An ecstasy of fumbling,
Fitting the clumsy helmets just in time;
But someone still was yelling out and stumbling
And floundering like a man in fire or lime...   (12)
Dim, through the misty panes and thick green light
As under a green sea, I saw him drowning.

In all my dreams, before my helpless sight,
He plunges at me, guttering, choking, drowning.   (16)
If in some smothering dreams you too could pace
Behind the wagon that we flung him in,
And watch the white eyes writhing in his face,
His hanging face, like a devil's sick of sin;   (20)
If you could hear, at every jolt, the blood
Come gargling from the froth-corrupted lungs,
Obscene as cancer, bitter as the cud
Of vile, incurable sores on innocent tongues, –   (24)
My friend, you would not tell with such high zest
To children ardent for some desperate glory,
The old Lie: Dulce et decorum est
Pro patria mori.   (28)

By Wilfred Owen (1893-1918).

Notes on the text:

Dulce Et Decorum Est is Latin for *It is sweet and right to die for your country.*

Line 3 – *flares* were rockets that burned brilliant white to show up targets

Line 4 – *distant rest* was the soldiers camp

Line 7 – *hoots* was the sound of shells

Line 9 – *Gas* meant poison gas shells

Line 12 – *lime* is a chalky substance that burns flesh

Line 13 – *panes* are the glass eyepieces in their gas helmets

Line 16 – *guttering* means flickering like a candle

Line 23 – *cud* is the regurgitated grass a cow coughs up

Line 25 – *zest* means enthusiasm

Line 26 – *ardent* means keen

This famous poem was written during the First World War (1914-1918) and describes the horror of war in the trenches on the Western Front in France. It was written by a British officer called Wilfred Owen, who was sadly killed in action a few days before the war ended in 1918. He was only 25 years old.

1. **Subject** – The poem is about the terror of war and the resultant death, destruction and waste of human life.

2. **Mood** – The overall feeling and atmosphere in the poem is one of exhaustion followed by terror when the gas shells fall.

3. **Tone** – The attitude of the poet towards the war is one of anger and cynicism. Wilfred Owen also makes use of dramatic irony. The supposed truth that it is good to die for your country is set against the reality and horror of war and pointless death in the trenches.

4. **Theme** – There is no real glory in war but only pain and pointless suffering.

5. **Moral** – The idea that is good to die for your country is a lie. We should learn this lesson from those who have truly experienced the horror of war. There is nothing glorious about it at all. It is destructive and pointless.

Exercise 4: 4

Examine this famous poem closely and use the five tools to explore its meaning:

Ozymandias

I met a traveller from an antique land
Who said: "Two vast and trunkless legs of stone
Stand in the desert. Near them on the sand,
Half sunk, a shattered visage lies, whose frown (4)
And wrinkled lip and sneer of cold command
Tell that its sculptor well those passions read
Which yet survive, stamped on these lifeless things,
The hand that mocked them and the heart that fed. (8)
And on the pedestal these words appear:
'My name is Ozymandias, King of Kings:
Look on my works, ye mighty, and despair!'
Nothing beside remains. Round the decay (12)
Of that colossal wreck, boundless and bare,
The lone and level sands stretch far away."

By Percy Bysshe Shelley (1792-1822).

Notes on the text:
Line 4 – *Visage* means face
Line 9 – *Pedestal* means stone on which something stands
Line 13 – *Colossal* means massive

Score

1-2) Subject: _____

_____

_____ (2 marks)

3-4) Mood: _____

_____

_____ (2 marks)

5-6) Tone: _____

_____

_____ (2 marks)

7-8) Theme: _____

_____

_____ (2 marks)

9-10) Moral: _____

_____

_____ (2 marks)

Chapter Five
COMPREHENSION QUESTIONS
1. Three Question Types

There are three different types of question that can be asked of any piece of text whether it be prose or poetry. All responses should be written in full sentences. These types of question assess a child's ability on three different levels.

These question types can be about:

1. **Factual Information** – This involves identifying a piece of obvious and straightforward factual information from the

text. The answer to the question is often directly contained or strongly inferred from within the text. This type of question only has one right answer. It is sometimes referred to as finding information 'on the line'. It may be necessary to quote from the text to support your answer.

2. **Contextual Understanding** – This requires an understanding of what precedes and follows the relevant word or portion of the text and the ability to decide on the meaning it conveys. Obtaining the correct answer usually involves more thought and the answer is not always obvious. This is often called finding the answer 'between the lines'. It is important to quote from the text to support your answer.

3. **Evaluative Opinion** – This comprises gaining an understanding of the whole passage and having the ability to summarise ideas, compare different texts, weigh up ideas and give an opinion, or make a value judgment based on the evidence given in the text. This is the most difficult of all the skills. It can be termed as seeking the answer 'beyond the lines'. It is important draw on evidence from the text to support your answer.

Example: Demonstrate the three types of question that require answers to do with factual information, contextual understanding and evaluative opinion by using this passage.

The Selfish Giant

Every afternoon, as they were coming from school, the children used to go and play in the Giant's garden.

It was a large lovely garden, with soft green grass. Here and there over the grass stood beautiful flowers like stars, and there were twelve peach-trees that in the spring-time broke out into

(4)

delicate blossoms of pink and pearl, and in the autumn bore rich fruit. The birds sat on the trees and sang so sweetly that the children used to stop their games in order to listen to them. (8)

"How happy we are here!" they cried to each other.

One day the Giant came back. He had been to visit his friend the Cornish ogre, and had stayed with him for seven years. After the seven years were over he had said all that he had to say for his (12) conversation was limited, and he determined to return to his own castle. When he arrived he saw the children playing in the garden.

"What are you doing here?" he cried in a very gruff voice, (16) and the children ran away.

"My own garden is my own garden," said the Giant; "any one can understand that, and I will allow nobody to play in it but myself." (20)
So he built a high wall all round it, and put up a notice-board.

TRESPASSERS
WILL BE
PROSECUTED (24)

He was a very selfish Giant.

The poor children had now nowhere to play. They tried to play on the road, but the road was very dusty and full of hard stones, and they did not like it. They used to wander round the high wall when their lessons were over, and talk about the beautiful garden inside.

"How happy we were there," they said to each other. (28)

Then the spring came, and all over the country there were little blossoms and little birds. Only in the garden of the Selfish Giant it was still winter. The birds did not care to sing in it as there were no children, and the trees forgot to blossom. Once a (32) flower put its head out from the grass, but when it saw the notice-board it was so sorry for the children that it slipped back into the ground again, and went off to sleep. The only people who were pleased were the snow and the frost. (36)

"Spring has forgotten this garden," they cried, "so we will live here all the year round."

By Oscar Wilde (1854-1900).

1. Factual Information

1) When did the children like to play in the Giant's garden?
2) Why had the Giant been away?

Answers:

1) The children played in the garden in the afternoon on their way home from school (lines 1-2).
2) The Giant had been away visiting his friend the Cornish ogre (lines 10-11).

2. Contextual Understanding

3) Explain why the children were so happy in the garden and the Giant was so angry on his return.
4) What were the consequences of the Giant's selfishness?

Answers:

3) The children loved the garden because it was very large and had soft grass to play on. It also had beautiful blossoming trees that bore fruit and the children loved to listen to the birds singing. The Giant was very angry because he was extremely selfish and would allow no one else to play in his garden.
4) The children were no longer able to play in the garden and were forced to play out on the road. Spring arrived for the whole country, but in the garden it remained winter.

3. Evaluative Opinion

5) What does this story teach us about selfish behaviour?

Answer:

5) It teaches us that those who act selfishly and do not share with others drive other people away. Such people

become lonely and sad, as everybody will eventually desert them. Since they are not kind to others, they do not receive kindness in return.

Exercise 5: 1

Read this famous passage on 'The Mad Hatter's Tea Party' from *Alice in Wonderland* by Lewis Carroll and answer the questions that have been set on three levels.

There was a table set out under a tree in front of the house, and the March Hare and the Hatter were having tea at it; a Dormouse was sitting between them, fast asleep.

The table was a large one, but the three were all crowded together at one corner of it. (4)

   "No room! No room!" they cried out when they saw Alice coming.

   "There's plenty of room!" said Alice indignantly, and she (8)
sat down in a large armchair at one end of the table.

   The Hatter opened his eyes very wide on hearing this, but all he said was, "Why is a raven like a writing-desk?"

   "I'm glad they've begun asking riddles – I believe I can (12)
guess that," she added aloud.

   "Do you mean that you think you can find out the answer to it?" said the March Hare.

   "Exactly so," said Alice. (16)

   "Then you should say what you mean," the March Hare went on.

   "I do," Alice hastily replied; "at least, at least I mean what I say – that's the same thing, you know." (20)

   "You might just as well say," added the Dormouse, which seemed to be talking in its sleep, "that 'I breathe when I sleep' is the same thing as 'I sleep when I breathe!'"

   "It is the same thing with you," said the Hatter, and he (24)
poured a little hot tea upon its nose.

The Dormouse shook its head impatiently and said, without opening its eyes, "Of course, of course; just what I was going to remark myself." (28)

"Have you guessed the riddle yet?" the Hatter said, turning to Alice again.

"No, I give it up," Alice replied. "What's the answer?"

"I haven't the slightest idea," said the Hatter. (32)

"Nor I," said the March Hare.

Alice gave a weary sigh. "I think you might do something better with the time," she said, "than wasting it in asking riddles that have no answers." (36)

"Take some more tea," the March Hare said to Alice, very earnestly.

"I've had nothing yet," Alice replied in an offended tone, "so I can't take more." (40)

"You mean you can't take less," said the Hatter; "it's very easy to take more than nothing."

At this, Alice got up and walked off. The Dormouse fell asleep instantly and neither of the others took the least notice (44) *of her going, though she looked back once or twice; the last time she saw them, they were trying to put the Dormouse into the teapot.*

"At any rate, I'll never go there again!" said Alice, as she (48) *picked her way through the wood. "It's the stupidest tea-party I ever was at in all my life!" Just as she said this, she noticed that one of the trees had a door leading right into it.*

"That's very curious!" she thought. "I think I may as (52) *well go in at once." And in she went.*

Once more she found herself in the long hall and close to the little glass table. Taking the little golden key, she unlocked the door that led into the garden. Then she set to work nibbling at (56) *the mushroom (she had kept a piece of it in her pocket) till she was about a foot high; then she walked down the little passage; and then, she found herself at last in the beautiful garden, among the bright flower-beds and the cool fountains.* (60)

By Lewis Carroll (1832-1898).

Factual Information

1) What was Alice very confident she could do? _____

_____

2) How did Alice make herself grow again? _____

_____

Contextual Understanding

3-4) Why did Alice say there was plenty of room at the table? _____

_____

_____ (2 marks)

5-6) Describe the things that were done to the sleeping dormouse? _____

_____

_____ (2 marks)

Evaluative Opinion

7-10) Explain why Alice was so frustrated with the Mad Hatter and the March Hare.

_____

_____

_____

_____

_____

_____

_____

_____(4 marks)   Score ☐

2. Comprehension Practice

Remember how to approach the text:

1. Is the text prose or poetry? Make this decision before you start to read and explore the passage.

2. When first encountering the text, whether it be prose or poetry, always remember to:
- read without 'voicing'
- read actively
- answer correctly in sentences

3. Prose is usually read once properly using the above method, but a second read can take place if there is time or the passage is relatively short. A careful first read often means this can be followed up by scanning through the passage for information.

4. Poetry normally requires more than one thorough read through as it contains 'heightened language'. Each word and line is very carefully constructed and this requires much closer observation.

5. Remember the three question types that deal with:
- Factual Information
- Contextual Understanding
- Evaluative Opinion

3. Prose Questions

This is reminder of what to look for in prose passages:

The first five questions should be addressed on the initial read:

1) Is it fiction or it non-fiction?
2) What form of prose is it?

3) What is the purpose of the writing?
4) What is it about?
5) What is distinctive about it?

The second five questions should be used to probe the passage on the next read or by scanning through the passage:

6) Where does it take place?
7) When does it take place?
8) Who is involved?
9) What happens?
10) Why does it happen?

Exercise 5: 2

Read this passage from *The Wind in the Willows* by Kenneth Grahame and answer the following questions:

"You knew it must come to this, sooner or later, Toad," the Badger explained severely. "You've disregarded all the warnings we've given you, you've gone on squandering the money your father left you, and you're getting us animals a (4) *bad name in the district by your furious driving and your smashes and your rows with the police. Independence is all very well, but we animals never allow our friends to make fools of themselves beyond a certain limit; and that limit* (8) *you've reached. Now, you're a good fellow in many respects, and I don't want to be too hard on you.*

I'll make one more effort to bring you to reason. You will come with me into the smoking-room, and there you will (12) *hear some facts about yourself; and we'll see whether you come out of that room the same Toad that you went in."*

He took Toad firmly by the arm, led him into the smoking-room, and closed the door behind them. (16)

"That's no good!" said the Rat contemptuously. "Talking to Toad'll never cure him. He'll say anything."

They made themselves comfortable in arm-chairs and waited (20)
patiently. Through the closed door they could just hear the
long continuous drone of the Badger's voice, rising and
falling in waves of oratory; and presently they noticed that
the sermon began to be punctuated at intervals by long-drawn
sobs, evidently proceeding from the bosom of Toad, who was (24)
a soft-hearted and affectionate fellow, very easily converted
– for the time being – to any point of view.

After some three-quarters of an hour the door opened, and
the Badger reappeared, solemnly leading by the paw a very (28)
limp and dejected Toad. His skin hung baggily about him,
his legs wobbled, and his cheeks were furrowed by the tears
so plentifully called forth by the Badger's moving discourse.

  "Sit down there, Toad," said the Badger kindly, pointing (32)
to a chair. "My friends," he went on, "I am pleased to inform
you that Toad has at last seen the error of his ways. He is truly
sorry for his misguided conduct in the past, and he has
undertaken to give up motor-cars entirely and for ever. I have (36)
his solemn promise to that effect."

  "That is very good news," said the Mole gravely.

  "Very good news indeed," observed the Rat dubiously,
"if only, if only." (40)

He was looking very hard at Toad as he said this, and could
not help thinking he perceived something vaguely resembling
a twinkle in that animal's still sorrowful eye.

  "There's only one thing more to be done," continued the (44)
gratified Badger. "Toad, I want you solemnly to repeat, before
your friends here, what you fully admitted to me in the
smoking-room just now. First, you are sorry for what you've
done, and you see the folly of it all?" (48)

There was a long, long pause. Toad looked desperately this
way and that, while the other animals waited in grave silence.
At last he spoke.

  "No!" he said, a little sullenly, but stoutly; "I'm not (52)
sorry. And it wasn't folly at all! It was simply glorious!"

"What?" cried the Badger, greatly scandalised. "You

backsliding animal, didn't you tell me just now, in there."

 "Oh, yes, yes, in there," said Toad impatiently. "I'd have (56)
said anything in there. You're so eloquent, dear Badger, and
so moving, and so convincing, and put all your points so
frightfully well, you can do what you like with me in there,
and you know it. (60)

 But I've been searching my mind since, and going over
things in it, and I find that I'm not a bit sorry or repentant
really, so it's no earthly good saying I am; now, is it?"

 "Then you don't promise," said the Badger, "never to (64)
touch a motor-car again?"

 "Certainly not!" replied Toad emphatically. "On the
contrary, I faithfully promise that the very first motor-car I
see, poop-poop! Off I go in it!" (68)

 "Told you so, didn't I?" observed the Rat to the Mole.

By Kenneth Grahame (1859-1932).

Factual Information

1) Which characters had gone to see Mr. Toad?

_____

2) Whose reputation was at stake if Toad kept misbehaving?

_____

3) How long did Badger spend alone with Toad? _____

_____

4) What is the reason Toad gives for almost being convinced
by Badger? _____

_____

5) What was Toad not going to give up no matter what
anybody said? _____

_____

Contextual Understanding

6-7) What does Badger say that shows he cares about Toad?

_____

_____ (2 marks)

8-9) Describe how Toad initially reacts to Badger's reprimand. _____

_____

_____ (2 marks)

10-11) Why was Badger so convinced he had won Toad over? _____

_____

_____ (2 marks)

12-13) Why was Rat suspicious about Toad's sincerity?

_____

_____

_____ (2 marks)

Evaluative Opinion

14-16) Comment on what kind of character Badger is. Use evidence from the text to support your arguments. _____

_____

_____

_____ (3 marks)

17-20) Was Toad a good or a bad character? Use evidence from the text to justify your opinion. _____

_____

_____

_____

_____

_____ (4 marks)   **Score**

4. Poetry Questions

This is reminder of what to look for in poetry passages:
Sound Devices • **Structure** • **Imagery** • **Meaning**

Exercise 5: 3

Read this poem called *Bat* by DH Lawrence and answer the following questions:

At evening, sitting on this terrace,
When the sun from the west, beyond Pisa, beyond the
    mountains of Carrara
Departs, and the world is taken by surprise ...

When the tired flower of Florence is in gloom beneath
    the glowing
Brown hills surrounding ...   (4)

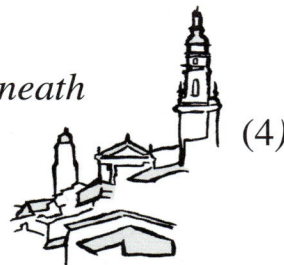

When under the arches of the Ponte Vecchio
A green light enters against stream, flush from the west,
    Against the current of obscure Arno ...   (8)

Look up, and you see things flying
Between the day and the night;
Swallows with spools of dark thread sewing the shadows together.

A circle swoop, and a quick parabola under the bridge arches   (12)
Where light pushes through;
A sudden turning upon itself of a thing in the air.
A dip to the water.

And you think: (16)
"The swallows are flying so late!"

Swallows?
Dark air-life looping
Yet missing the pure loop ...   (20)
A twitch, a twitter, an elastic shudder in flight
And serrated wings against the sky,

Like a glove, a black glove thrown up at the light,
And falling back. (24)

Never swallows!
Bats!

The swallows are gone.

At a wavering instant the swallows gave way to bats (28)
By the Ponte Vecchio ...
Changing guard.

Bats, and an uneasy creeping in one's scalp
As the bats swoop overhead! (32)
Flying madly.

Pipistrello!
Black piper on an infinitesimal pipe.
Little lumps that fly in air and have voices indefinite, (36)
wildly vindictive;

Wings like bits of umbrella.

Bats!
Creatures that hang themselves up like an old rag, to sleep; (40)
And disgustingly upside down.

Hanging upside down like rows of disgusting old rags
And grinning in their sleep.
Bats! (44)

In China the bat is symbol for happiness.

Not for me!

By DH Lawrence (1885-1930).

Factual Information

1) Where is the writer of the poem? _____

_____

2) Is this poem written in formal verse or free verse?

_____

3) Identify the two line numbers where anaphora occurs.

_____

4) What does the poet mistakenly think he sees flying through the air? _____

_____

5) How do the Chinese view bats? _____

_____

Contextual Understanding

6-7) Write down two examples of the use of similes in this poem. _____

_____

_____

_____ (2 marks)

8-9) Identify two metaphors the poet uses to describe how bats fly. _____

_____

_____

_____ (2 marks)

10-11) Identify two examples of alliteration from the poem.

_____

_____

_____ (2 marks)

12-13) The writer uses one very specific metaphor for

Florence and another very specific metaphor for the bat itself. What are these two metaphors? _____

_____

_____ (2 marks)

Evaluative Opinion

14-16) What is the mood (feeling or atmosphere) the poet wishes to create at the beginning of this poem and how does it change? _____

_____

_____

_____

_____

_____ (3 marks)

17-20) Comment on what the author feels about bats (consider how the tone of the poem changes midway). Use evidence from the poem to support your answer.

_____

_____

_____

_____

_____

_____ (4 marks)   **Score**

ae

Answers

Chapter One
Basic Approaches to Text
Exercise 1: 1a

1) Prose – An extract from *Bleak House* by Charles Dickens (1812-1870).

2) Poetry – An extract from *The Pied Piper of Hamelin* by Robert Browning (1812-1889).

3) Poetry – An extract from *Bitter for Sweet* by Christina Rossetti (1830-1894).

4) Prose – An extract from *Conversation about Christmas* by Dylan Thomas (1914-1953).

5) Poetry – An extract from *When You Are Old* by William Butler Yeats (1865-1939).

Exercise 1: 1b

6) Fiction – An extract from *The Wizard of Oz* by Frank L Baum (1856-1919).

7) Non-fiction – An extract from *Anne Frank's Diary* by Anne Frank (1929-1945).

8) Fiction – An extract from *The Tale of Peter Rabbit* by Beatrix Potter (1866-1943).

9) Non-fiction – A biographical extract from *The Royal Museums Greenwich* website about Horatio Nelson.

10) Fiction – An extract from *The War of the Worlds* by HG Wells (1866-1946).

Exercise 1: 2

1) Persuasive – A 1953 advertisement for Charles Antell, Incorporated's Fastabs tablets.

2) A play script – An extract from *Pygmalion* by George Bernard Shaw (1856-1950).

3) Narrative – An extract from *Gulliver's Travels* by Jonathan Swift (1667-1745).

4) Reportage – Newspaper Headline from the *Daily Mail*, 4th September 1939.

5) Diary – An extract from *Samuel Pepys Diary* on the Great Fire of London, 2nd September 1666.

6) Factual – Definition of Football from *The 1911 Encyclopedia Britannica*.

7) Letter – An extract of a letter from Mary, Queen of Scots written at Fotheringay Castle to her brother-in-law, King Henry of France on 8th February 1587, just prior to her execution.

8) Biography – An extract about Wolfgang Amadeus Mozart from *First Studies in Music Biography* (1901) by Thomas Tapper (1864-1958).

9) Narrative – An extract from *The Last of the Mohicans* by James Fenimore Cooper (1789-1851).

10) Persuasive – A Vapex advertisement from the 1930s.

Answers

Exercise 1: 3

1) Lyric poetry – An extract from *The Wild Swans at Coole* by William Butler Yeats (1865-1939).

2) Narrative poetry – An extract from *The Charge of the Light Brigade* by Alfred Lord Tennyson (1809-1892).

3) Lyric poetry – An extract from *A Noiseless Patient Spider* by Walt Whitman (1819-1892).

4) Narrative poetry – An extract from *The Listeners* by Walter de la Mare (1873-1956).

5) Lyric poetry – A Limerick by Edward Lear (1812-1888).

6) Lyric poetry – A Haiku poem by Matsuo Basho (1644-1694).

7) Narrative poetry – An extract from *A Smuggler's Song* by Rudyard Kipling (1865-1936).

8) Lyric poetry – An extract from *Death the Leveller* by James Shirley (1596-1666).

9) Narrative poetry – *How doth the Little Crocodile* by Lewis Carroll (1832-1898).

10) Narrative poetry – The opening extract from *A Ballad of John Silver* by John Masefield (1878-1967).

Chapter Two
Probing the Text
Exercise 2: 1

1) To inform – This is an extract from *Queen Victoria's private journals* for June 28th 1838, the day of her coronation.

2) To describe – This is an extract from *An Inland Voyage* (through the Golden Valley) by Robert Louis Stevenson (1850-1894).

3) To entertain – *The Big Baboon* is a humorous poem by Hilaire Belloc (1870-1953).

4) To explain – An extract from the *Boy Scouts' Handbook* of the Boy Scouts of America (1911).

5) To persuade – An extract from the *I have a Dream* speech given in Washington DC by the civil rights activist, Dr Martin Luther King on the 28th August 1963.

6) To entertain – The opening extract from *Alice in Wonderland* by Lewis Carroll (1832-1898).

7) To inform – The opening excerpt from the Prime Minister, Neville Chamberlain's *Declaration of War with Germany* speech broadcast over BBC radio on the 3rd September 1939.

Answers

8) To explain – An ancient Roman recipe for *Roast Wild Boar* recorded by Apicius in 330.

9) To persuade – An advertisement for Chamberlain's Cough Remedy – undated.

10) To describe – An extract from *Little Dorrit* by Charles Dickens (1812-1870) which describes Amy Dorrit's eccentric uncle.

Exercise 2: 2

One mark for each sentence with a relevant point

1-3) This passage is about Geppetto, a simple carpenter who makes a puppet out of a lump of wood and names him Pinocchio after a family he knows. As he carves the eyes they appear to move and the nose keeps growing even when he cuts it off. The mouth laughs at him until he shouts for it to stop.

4-5) It is distinctive because it is a magical story where a wooden puppet comes to life. Geppetto oddly becomes sad when the Pinocchio seems to misbehave as he appears to regard him as his son.

6-8) This passage is about the bombing carried out by the German air force in London during the Second World War. During the day there are five air raid warnings but the bombing only begins during the night. At first very little happens but eventually six huge explosions are heard.

9-10) It is distinctive because it describes the moment when the German air force begins bombing the civilian population in London rather than just military targets. It shockingly records six gigantic explosions across two districts, no doubt killing many people.

Chapter Three
Analysing Prose
Exercise 3: 1

Only award 1 mark for a partial answer

Where does it take place?

1-2) **Identify the location or locations that are mentioned** – It begins inside the Earnshaw home but then the master talks of his visit to the poor streets of Liverpool.

3-4) **Give a brief description of this place or places** – The Earnshaw home is not described but we can assume it is wealthy household. It obviously contrasts sharply with the streets of Liverpool where he has found a destitute and starving child.

Answers

When does it take place?

5-6) **Identify the period of history, e.g. modern day or sometime in the past** – It seems to be a long time ago as people in Britain are not as poor as this anymore and children are better cared for. The type of language – e.g. use of 'master' and 'mistress' seems old fashioned. The story takes place more than one hundred years ago.

7-8) **Specify the time of day, season, year or time period over which it takes place** – It is the evening as the master has spent the day in Liverpool and he is very tired.

Who is involved?

9-10) **Identify the key characters. Is there a 1ˢᵗ person or 3ʳᵈ person narrator?** Mr Earnshaw and his wife, and Miss Cathy, one of their children, and the young boy appear to be the main characters. There is a 1ˢᵗ person narrator who appears to be an eyewitness to the events.

11-12) **Briefly describe key features of these characters** – The Earnshaw family seems to be wealthy and privileged. Mrs Earnshaw appears to be a strong character who is protective of her family. Mr Earnshaw seems to be a compassionate man as he brings the destitute boy home. The dark haired boy is dirty, hungry and barely able to speak. Cathy or Catherine appears to be around the same age as the boy and is keenly interested in him.

What happens?

13-14) **Summarise the main actions that occur** – The master of the house, Mr Earnshaw, to the horror of his wife has returned from Liverpool with a homeless gypsy boy whom he found on the streets. Miss Cathy, the oldest child in the family is one of the closest observers and the gypsy boy is compared with her. The boy is to be washed and fed and allowed to sleep in the same room as the other children.

15-16) **What is the key event that takes place and why?** – The disagreement over what should be done with the gypsy child.

Why does it happen?

17-18) **What does this event tell us about the story?** – This might be a key event in the story as a destitute boy has been brought into the house, which may upset the settled life of the family.

19-20) **Do these characters tell us anything about the story?** – The interest shown by Cathy for the gypsy boy seems to be an indication that this relationship will develop further as they grow up.

© 2013 Stephen Curran

Answers

Exercise 3: 2

Where questions have 2 marks, only award 1 mark for a partial answer.

1) Fiction

2) Narrative

3) To entertain

4) This passage is about a child called Little Nell who lives with her grandfather in an old curiosity shop. Little Nell is happy until her grandfather falls very sick. She soon learns they are to become poor, as they no longer own their house.

5) It is distinctive because the heroine of the story is a little girl who is brave and intelligent. As a small child she comes to know that they are destitute and feels the full force of something only adults normally deal with.

Where does it take place?

6) **Identify the location or locations that are mentioned** – The old curiosity shop and its rooms.

7-8) **Give a brief description of this place or places** – The shop is tucked away in a quirky corner of the town. It is full of weird and bizarre objects and antiques. The living rooms are old, dark and dismal.

When does it take place?

9) **Identify the period of history, e.g. modern day or sometime in the past** – This story is probably set over 100 years ago as Charles Dickens is the author. Children are not left destitute in modern day Britain as this story indicates.

10) **Specify the time of day, season, year or time period over which it takes place** – There is no specific time period but it occurs over a period of some weeks.

Who is involved?

11) **Identify the key characters. Is there a 1st person or 3rd person narrator?** – The key characters are the child, Little Nell and her grandfather. There is an anonymous 3rd person narrator telling the story.

12-13) **Briefly describe the key features of these characters** – Little Nell is cheerful, happy, of gentle spirit and very loving. Her grandfather is also very loving and very responsible. He worries so much about their problem he becomes very ill.

What happens?

14-15) **Summarise the main actions that occur** – Little Nell lives a happy but solitary and dull life at the old curiosity shop with her grandfather. The old man becomes increasingly troubled about something. He then grows very ill with fever and at this point Little Nell discovers they no longer own their house.

Answers

16) **Identify the key event that takes place** – Little Nell learns the devastating truth that they have become very poor. They are destitute and soon to be made homeless.

Why does it happen?

17-18) **What does this event or events tell us about the story?** – The impoverishment of Little Nell and her grandfather is the main problem the characters will have to solve. They are faced with almost insurmountable difficulties and will need great courage and resourcefulness to deal with them.

19-20) **Do these characters tell us anything about the story?** – The opening clearly establishes Little Nell as the heroine even though she is so young. There is also a great bond of love between this child and her grandfather and this must be significant to the story.

Chapter Four
Analysing Poetry
Exercise 4: 1
Only award one mark if there is an insufficient answer.

1-2) **Alliteration** – This occurs in line 1 – *dead, my dearest,* line 2 – *sing no sad songs for me,* line 5 *green grass* and line 9 – *see the shadows.*

3-4) **Assonance** – This occurs at the end of line rhymes in lines 2, 4 and 5 – *me, tree* and *me,* lines 6 and 8 – *wet* and *forget,* lines 10 and 12 – *rain* and *pain* and lines 14 and 16 – *set* and *forget*

5-6) **Consonance** – This occurs in line 6 – showers and dewdrops and in line 8 – *wilt forget.*

7-8) **Onomatopoeia** – In line 2 – *sing* and *songs* and in line 6 – *Showers* carry the sounds of the things they describe.

9-10) **Anaphora** – In lines 9-11, *I shall not see the shadows, I shall not see the rain, I shall not hear the nightingale* there is a repetition of *I shall not.* Also, in lines 7-8, *And if thou wilt, remember; And if thou wilt, forget* there is a repetition of *And if thou wilt.*

Exercise 4: 2
Only award one mark if there is an insufficient answer.

1-2) **Type of Verse** – The poem is in formal verse and there is a pattern of rhyme, verse length and meter.

3-4) **Stanzas** – There are three stanzas of four lines each (quatrains).

Answers

5-6) **Rhymes** – In stanza 1 and 3 the 2ⁿᵈ and 4ᵗʰ line rhyme and in stanza 2, the 2ⁿᵈ and 3ʳᵈ line rhyme. It can also be written as ABCB, ABBC, ABCB.

7-8) **Rhythm or Meter** – The poem has a clear rhythm and some lines are in iambic pentameter. Although it does not follow the same metrical pattern throughout, the overall rhythmical effect is of an even beat.

9-10) **Punctuation and Line Breaks** – All lines have caesurae and there is little other punctuation. This gives the poem a very even and flowing feel even though the lines are of variable length.

Exercise 4: 3

Only award one mark if there is an insufficient answer.

This poem is a detailed observation of a bird foraging for food followed by the attempt of the author to offer it food, which in turn provokes the bird to fly away.

1-2) **Metaphor** – The more obvious metaphors include: *velvet head* – line 8, *He unrolled his feathers and rowed him…* – lines 15-16. A less obvious metaphor occurs in lines 5-6 – *And then he drank a dew From a convenient grass*. The word *grass* is a play on *glass*. It is as if the poet wants us to think of the bird drinking its dew from a glass just like a human might drink water.

3-4) **Personification** – Throughout the poem the bird is referred to as *he* and is given human characteristics. *He* drinks as from *a convenient grass* – as if from a *glass* like a human. *He* hops to a wall *to let a beetle pass*. His eyes glance around cautiously as if *he* is afraid and he knows *he is in danger.*

5-6) **Simile** – There are two similes in the poem. The poet says the bird's *eyes… looked like frightened beads* – line 11. Another is, *He stirred his velvet head like one in danger* – lines 12-13.

7-8) **Symbols** – The last part of the poem (lines 16-20) is highly symbolic. The ocean represents the sky as the bird takes flight and its as if its wings softly row this ocean like oars. As the ocean parts the white surf is like silver, but even shinier than that found in a *seam* of rock where it is mined. Butterflies leaping from the banks and skirting the water also symbolise the bird's flight.

9-10) **Hyperbole** – The comparison of the bird's wings with oars that are going to row a great ocean is very effective exaggeration that makes the bird's sudden flight seem very dramatic.

Exercise 4: 4

Only award one mark if there is an insufficient answer.

This poem is a 14-line sonnet in iambic pentameter. It describes the remains of a

Answers

statue of *Ozymandius*. This is the Greek name for Ramses II, the 13th century BC King of Egypt.

1-2) **Subject** – This poem is about *Ozymandius*, a great ruler who was once proclaimed by his followers as *King of Kings* – line 10.

3-4) **Mood** – The mood of the poem is serious and sombre as the traveller recounts the ultimate and shocking fate of *Ozymandius* who was once all-powerful.

5-6) **Tone** – The author displays a questioning and mocking attitude as he reflects on the fate of *Ozymandius* as related by the traveller. Shelley makes use of dramatic irony by contrasting the glory and power of Ozymandius when he was alive with the fact that all that remains of him now is a broken statue.

7-8) **Theme** – This is contained in the words *'Look on my works, ye mighty, and despair! Nothing beside remains.'* – lines 11-12. No matter how great a leader may proclaim himself to be, death will claim him one day and nothing but ruins will remain to commemorate him.

9-10) **Moral** – The poet is making people aware that they too will face the same fate no matter how successful they have become and that perhaps they should reflect on *Ozymandius* when they are tempted to boast of their powers and achievements.

Chapter Five
Comprehension Questions
Exercise 5: 1

1) Alice was very confident she could answer the Mad Hatter's riddle (lines 12-13).

2) Alice made herself grow again by nibbling on the mushroom she had kept in her pocket (lines 56-57).

3-4) The Mad Hatter and the March Hare were crowded together at one corner of the table. Alice was able to sit in an armchair at the end of the table, as it was very large.

5-6) The dormouse had tea poured onto its nose after it made a silly comment. Later the Mad Hatter and the March Hare try to stuff it into the teapot.

7-10) Alice was frustrated with the Mad Hatter and the March Hare because they told her there was no room at the table when there clearly was. The Mad Hatter also asked Alice a riddle she could not answer. When challenged by Alice, the Mad Hatter said he had no idea what the answer was either. Alice was also asked if she wanted more tea even though she had been offered none in the first place.

Answers

Exercise 5: 2

1) Badger, Mole and Rat had paid a visit to Toad.

2) The animals in the district were getting a bad name and Toad was making a fool of himself (lines 4-5).

3) Badger spent three-quarters of an hour alone with Toad (line 27).

4) Toad said he was almost taken in by Badger because he was eloquent and convincing (lines 57-58).

5) Toad made it clear he would never give up motorcars and would take the very first opportunity he could to drive one again (lines 66-68).

6-7) Badger says that as a friend he does not want to see Toad making a fool of himself. He thinks he is basically a good fellow, does not wish to be too hard on him, and wants to give him one more chance.

8-9) Toad sobs as Badger reprimands him. As he emerges from the smoking room he looks limp and dejected, his legs wobble and he is still tearful.

10-11) Badger says that Toad had understood the error of his ways and was truly sorry for his past conduct. He claims Toad had solemnly promised to give up motorcars forever.

12-13) Rat believes Toad will say anything under pressure and a talking to will not cure him. As Badger announces the success of his interview with Toad, Rat notices a twinkle in Toad's eye that suggests he is not being sincere.

14-16) Badger is the leader of the group and is an impressive speaker. He is also caring and loyal towards his friends, even when they misbehave. However, Badger is gullible and easily deceived, since he is taken in by Toad's apparent repentant behaviour and empty promises.

17-20) Toad is clearly bad, but is also a likeable rogue. He is wealthy but has been squandering his inheritance on a wild and out of control lifestyle. He drives in a crazy manner, is deceptive, manipulative, gets into rows with the police and will say anything to get out of trouble. Toad is fiercely independent and wants to enjoy himself whatever the cost, even if it means losing his friends.

Exercise 5: 3

1) The writer of the poem is sitting on a terrace in Florence.

2) This poem is written in free verse.

3) Anaphora occurs in lines 2 and 4 where the poet starts with *When* in both lines.

4) The poet mistakenly thinks he sees swallows flying through the air.

Answers

5) The Chinese believe bats are a symbol of happiness.

6-7) The poet uses similes to describe the bats by saying they are *like a glove, a black glove thrown up at the light* (line 23), they have *wings like bits of umbrella* (line 38) and they hang upside down to sleep *like rows of disgusting old rags* (lines 40-42) Note – only two out of three similes are needed for 2 marks.

8-9) The poet uses various metaphors to describe the bats in flight such as *spools of dark thread sewing the shadows together* (line 11); *a quick parabola under the bridge arches* (line 12 – a mathematical term for a type of curve); *an elastic shudder in flight and serrated wings* (lines 21-22) and *little lumps that fly in air* (line 36). Note – only two out of three metaphors are needed for 2 marks.

10-11) Alliteration is mainly seen in line 11 with the repeated use of the *s* sound – *Shadows with spools of dark thread sewing the shadows together*. It is also used in line 4 where the *f* sound is repeated – *flower of Florence*; in line 21 where the *t* sound is repeated – *a twitch, a twitter*; and in line 37 where the *l* sound is repeated in *Little lumps* (only two out of four examples of alliteration are needed for 2 marks).

12-13) The writer uses metaphors to compare *Florence* with a *tired flower* (line 4) and as the darkness falls he describes the bats as *little lumps that fly* (line 36).

14-16) The mood at the beginning of the poem is very calm and peaceful. The poet creates a scene of great beauty: the disappearing sun over the horizon, the fading light over Florence, the brown hills and the green light shining on the river through the arches. The mood becomes eerie as the poet describes the sudden appearance of bats, their scary and disturbing flight patterns and their ugly features.

17-20) The poet does not seem to like bats and finds them very scary. At first he is fascinated by what he thinks are swallows but as soon as he realises they are bats he seems alarmed. He says they cause *an uneasy creeping in one's scalp* (line 31), their voices seem *wildly vindictive* (line 37) and they hang *upside down like disgusting old rags* (lines 40-42) and are *grinning in their sleep* (line 43). His final comment, *Not for me!* (line 46) in reference to the Chinese idea of the bat as a symbol of happiness, suggests he finds bats in some way quite revolting.

PROGRESS CHARTS

Exercise	Score	%
1: 1		
1: 2		
1: 3		
2: 1		
2: 2		
3: 1		
3: 2		
4: 1		
4: 2		
4: 3		
4: 4		
5: 1		
5: 2		
5: 3		

Overall Score

Overall Percentage

%

CERTIFICATE OF

ACHIEVEMENT

This certifies

_____

has successfully completed

Key Stage 2
Comprehension
WORKBOOK **1**

Overall percentage
score achieved

%

Comment _____

_____

Signed _____

(teacher/parent/guardian)

Date _____